D0985041

NOV 2 9

GAYLORD   PRINTED IN U.S.A.

GOKHALE

A MAURYA.

TWAYNE'S
RULERS AND STATESMEN OF THE WORLD
SERIES

Hans L. Trefousse, Brooklyn College
General Editor

Tom B. Jones, University of Minnesota
Editor, Ancient World

ASOKA MAURYA

(TROW 3)

Asoka Maurya

By BALKRISHNA GOVIND GOKHALE

Professor of History and Director
Asian Studies Program, Wake Forest College

Twayne Publishers, Inc. :: New York

To
The Memory Of My Teachers

DHARMANAND KOSAMBI
CHINTAMAN VINAYAK JOSHI
NARAYAN KESHAV BHAGWAT
REV. HENRY HERAS, S.J.

Preface

Asoka Maurya is one of the most fascinating personalities of Indian history. His aversion to war, his solicitude for the welfare of his people, both in this world and the next, and his frankness in claiming successes as well as in admitting failures in his appointed tasks, have endeared him to all those interested in the history of India.

Books on Asoka are indeed many. Ever since the decipherment of his inscriptions Asoka has been a subject of interpretation and reinterpretation. His edicts have been critically analyzed, and Buddhist literature in Pali and Sanskrit has been searched for information on this extraordinary monarch. As a result, an impressive collection of facts and conjectures has been gathered in the course of Asokan studies over the past half a century and more. This work attempts to collate the available information on Asoka and present it in historically intelligible terms. But the work is more than a mere collection of previously known facts. I have attempted a study in some depth of the personality of Asoka. Currently there are two prevailing trends in Asokan studies. One is to minimize the importance of Buddhism in Asoka's life and public policy. The other is to denigrate Buddhist literature as a source of historical information on Asoka. I dissent from both. For me Asoka is as much a Buddhist as an Indian emperor. I hold that Buddhism was a significant attempt at a new interpretation of the Indic experience and was largely responsible for the development of the Asokan personality. Asoka's problem, as I see it, was to bring about a synthesis of two divergent philosophies, those of Kautalya and the Buddha. The Kautalyan philosophy was a doctrine of political power, its necessity, its security and growth. The Buddha spoke essentially of human greatness beyond the grandeur of political power. As an emperor Asoka was an heir to Kautalya's philosophy; as a Buddhist he had to heed the preachings of the Master. His life was an experiment in resolving the apparent conflict between the two demands made on him. Viewed in this perspective Asoka is much more significant to me as a thinker and a moralist in action than merely a powerful emperor or efficient administrator. He was also the creator of a new age whose achievements are recorded not only in religious chronicles but also in art, diplomacy and statecraft. In all these respects Asoka stands head and shoulders above the galaxy of Indian kings and belongs in the company of the great rulers of the world.

I have mainly relied on Asoka's inscriptions and Buddhist literature in Pali and Sanskrit for my information. I have also drawn rather copiously on the works of the many great scholars, to whom I am grateful. I have endeavored to give my own interpretations at certain points in the unfolding of the Asokan story, and if the work enables the reader to understand something of this great personality, I will feel amply rewarded.

Many people have helped me in my work. My thanks are due to Mrs. Harold L. Grogan, Secretary, Asian Studies Program, for her ungrudging assistance in typing and many other chores; Sylvia Bledsoe for drawing the map; Mrs. Cornelius C. Mertes and Mrs. Richard K. Gardner of the College Library for assistance in securing materials; Mr. S. D. Gaikwad, Tutor in History, Siddharth College of Arts and Science, Bombay, for assistance from libraries in India; Mr. Charles H. Babcock, Sr. of the Mary Reynolds Babcock Foundation and Drs. Harold W. Tribble and Edwin G. Wilson, President and Dean, Wake Forest College, for their interest in my work. Finally my wife, Beena Gokhale, has been my helpful critic and has rendered me assistance in checking the text and preparing the index and to her my appreciative thanks.

B. G. GOKHALE

Wake Forest College
Winston-Salem, N. C.

Contents

Chronology

All dates are B.C. With the exception of Alexander's invasion all dates are approximate.

For list of abbreviations see page 172.

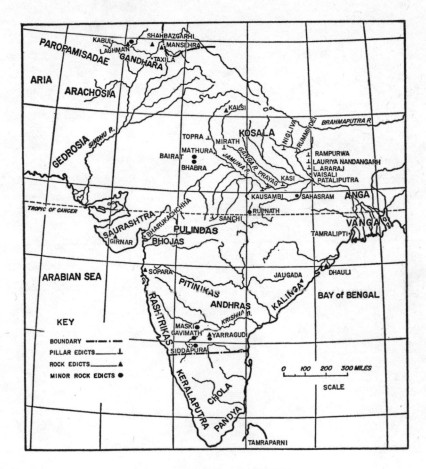

The EMPIRE of ASOKA

CHAPTER I

Birth of an Empire

BRILLIANT AND MEMORABLE IN THE PAGEANT OF HISTORY, THE third century B.C. was an age of empires and an era of cultural growth. While Rome dueled with Carthage in the West, Latin literature was born, and Archimedes of Syracuse raised science and mathematics to new heights. At the other end of the Mediterranean, amid the struggles of the great Hellenistic kingdoms, Aristarchus and Hipparchus, Euclid and Eratosthenes, Zeno and Epicurus brought significant new ideas into the world. Still farther east, a resplendent India, unified and prosperous under the Mauryas, attained its zenith during the reign of Asoka, the warrior, conqueror, penitent pilgrim, and kingly philosopher whose deeds provided material for a whole new chapter in the history of Buddhism and of India.

It was the year 269 B.C. when Asoka came to the peacock throne of the Mauryas.[1] His father had been emperor before him, while his grandfather, Chandragupta, had founded the Maurya Empire in 322, only a few months after the death of Alexander the Great. There was a connnection between Alexander and Chandragupta, for, though less directly than the Ptolemies or the Seleucids but nevertheless to a certain degree, the Mauryas owed their empire to Alexander's conquests.

Empires are often the offspring of revolutions, and no less than three distinct upheavals had paved the way for the rule of the Mauryas. First, a social revolution had occurred in India that was connected with the growth of commodity production, trade, and merchant capital. An important consequence of this social change was the rise of the "protestant" sects, Buddism and Jainism, with their new ethical and social norms addressed to man instead of tribes and castes.

A second revolution had been generated by the incursion into northwest India of the Achaemenian Persian and Greco-Macedonian empires. These introduced into the country new types of imperial and military organization along with a new internationalism.

The third revolution was a dynastic one that began in Magadha (northern Bihar) in the middle of the sixth century B.C. and was subsequently extended over major parts of India by the end of the fourth century.

These three revolutions were partly contemporary and to some extent interrelated. This will become apparent as we consider the details of each in turn.

I

The sixth century B.C. was a time of far-reaching social changes and a "time of troubles" [2] for the tribal oligarchies of northern India. Large parts of the Gangetic area had come under settled agriculture, and land was slowly becoming private property, although not a commodity to be freely bought and sold. This new form of property and the advent of plough-cultivation[3] created surpluses of commodities that could be profitably exchanged in the growing market towns of the region. The growth of surpluses brought into existence a new social class, a class of prosperous merchants and wealthy bankers, whose transactions were greatly facilitated by the discovery of metals, especially copper and iron, within easy reach of the emerging state of Magadha. Progress was hampered by a tribal economy that fettered productive relations, while the division of the land into innumerable oligarchic republics and petty kingdoms hindered the free flow of trade and commerce. Moreover, the frequent wars between these numerous states made both life and property insecure, and it was in the interest of the new social class to support the growth of large and powerful kingdoms, and even to create, if possible, an empire.

The most important fact indicated by our evidence is that the cash nexus was becoming the basis of economic relations in the second half of the sixth century B.C. The Buddhist books, our main source of information for this age, make a common mention of currency; everything now, from the price of a dead rat to that of a holiday in Banaras, tended to be counted in terms of cash.[4] The growth of the cash economy greatly accelerated trade and commerce, which came to hold a decisive superiority over other forms of property-creating institutions. The new social hero was neither the Brahmin nor the Kshatriya, the traditional priestly and warrior classes, but the merchant and the banker, the greatest of whom was Anathapindika of Shravasti. The changing economic structure is well illustrated by the story of how this great banker bought a plot of land from the prince Jeta to build a monastery for the Buddha. It seems Anathapindika (the name itself is suggestive of the rather nondescript social origin of our merchant-hero) had taken a fancy to a pleasance owned by the prince Jeta. He went to the prince and asked how much the plot would cost. The prince replied, "As many pieces of copper coins as the whole plot would take to cover." This was a fantastic price, for the purchasing power of the *karshapana* (a square punch-marked coin of copper or silver) was great and the plot was fairly extensive, a bamboo forest as it was called, and would take thousands of these small coins to cover its surface. But without a second thought the price was accepted, and the banker promptly ordered cartloads of coins to be brought and spread over the ground. Over this plot was later built a monastery where the Buddha spent many rain-retreats.[5]

This story clearly shows that trade and commerce had brought into being a new and powerful social class of merchants and bankers. Most of the professions were organized into guilds and localized in certain well-defined areas. Gradually these guilds of merchants and artisans gathered considerable power in their hands. They began to be recognized by the state as important organs of society, and their laws were respected by kings who gladly gave the guilds representation at their courts. The guilds functioned in such a wide variety of ways that they controlled not only the professional aspects of a person's life but also intervened in personal matters to some extent. They received deposits of money and gave loans; they accepted responsibilities for the construction and maintenance of public works; and they raised armed bands of mercenary soldiers for the protection of their properties. They ensured the quality of goods manufactured by their members and controlled prices; they even required that before a member's wife joined a Buddhist monastery the guild's permission should be secured.[6]

The development of trade and commerce was based on the growth of numerous well-recognized trade routes crisscrossing far-flung parts of the country. Magadha was gradually becoming the hub of this extensive commerce and was well-connected with parts of western, central, northern, and northwestern India.[7] Riverine and seaports like Banaras, Kaushambi (Kosam near Allahabad), Surat, Broach, and Sopara (near Bombay) were beginning to flourish, and the Tales of the Buddha (*Jatakas* or Birth-Stories of the Buddha) are replete with references to long caravans of bullock-carts wending their way across forest and desert trails with their precious merchandise. More and more it was obvious that merchant capital was going to dominate the economic and social life of the country.

This was also an age of colonization of hitherto sparsely populated areas. New land was being brought into cultivation, and the forests were receding rapidly before the spread of new colonies of settlers and husbandmen. This process needed new forms of labor. Slavery, which was known and practiced then, could have been an obvious answer to this pressing problem of labor supply. But slavery had disadvantages, for it involved a continuous use of force and created possibilities of counterrebellions by the slaves. The solution was found through an increasing use of the *Shudra* class. These Shudras came in part from the elements reduced to slavery by the invading Aryans from among the conquered non-Aryan population, though the presence of an Aryan element among the Shudra class cannot be altogether ruled out.[8] The creation of a servile class like that of the Shudras, who became the fourth caste in Brahmanical society later, was the solution found by ancient India for minimizing the use of institutional slavery in economic life. The Shudra was not a slave but was nevertheless firmly bound to productive work by tradition and custom, later codified into inexorable and almost unchanging Brahmanical law codes like those of Manu, Gautama, and Narada. Tradition barred the Shudra from acquiring knowledge and becoming a priest like the Brahmin, or bearing arms like the Kshatriya, or taking to trade and commerce like the Vaishya. His duty was to serve the three higher social orders. The emergence of the Shudra provided society with a numerous, unarmed, and servile laboring class that could ungrudgingly bear the burden of performing the most arduous and economically productive tasks and thus aid in the emergence of a new and comparatively affluent society.

These changes were taking place within Indian society for over three centuries. The pace of change in the various parts of the country was necessarily different, but gradually the pattern was becoming universal, affecting all strata of society in almost all areas. This ever expanding period of social and economic change was certainly a necessary prelude to the rise of an imperial political order.

These far-reaching social and economic changes also have their echoes in the rise of new "protestant" sects like Buddhism and Jainism. From about 1000 B.C. there had developed in northern India a religion based on elaborate ritual requiring the assistance of a priesthood that had begun to claim many extravagant social privileges. This ritual had become increasingly irrelevant for the large masses of the people, the new ruling classes, merchants, and peasants. It was also economically wasteful as it involved the slaughter of numerous cattle, the basis of a pastoral and agricultural economy. In Magadha and the adjoining areas, this Brahmanism met with stubborn resistance as much from the new monarchies as from the republican oligarchies. The Buddha (*circa* 567-486 B.C.) and Mahavira, the founder of Jainism (*circa* 561-490 B.C.), came from oligarchic tribes. At that time the world of these tribes was increasingly threatened by the rising monarchies, and the prophets could do little to save their tribes from defeat and annihilation at the hands of the new and aggressive monarchs of the times. The Buddha and Mahavira preached in Magadha and found support from the merchant and Shudra classes and were also on very friendly terms with contemporary kings. It is not necessary for us to go into the details of their lives and activities at this point; it is sufficient to emphasize that these new creeds not only rejected ritualism and mysticism but also preached a certain equality of spiritual opportunities for all men regardless of race, tribe, or caste.[9] They insisted upon the primacy of ethical values over mere intellectual speculation and protested against the domination of the Brahmanical priest. In this, they gave expression to the spiritual and social urges of the new classes generated by the economic revolution.

II

Let us now turn to the second of the three revolutions that preceded the rise of the Maurya Empire. This revolution came in the shape of the West Asian intrusion represented by the

Achaemenid and Hellenic empires which included, among their far-flung domains, parts of northwestern India. Like Magadha, the heartland of the Maurya Empire, the land of Persia had also witnessed far-reaching social and economic changes some three centuries before the rise of the Achaemenian empire. The major actors in this drama, the Medes and Persians, are first noticed by history in the ninth century B.C. as vassals of Assyria. It was among the Medes in the sixth century B.C. that the prophet Zoroaster first preached his message. The Persians proved to be more receptive to him, and like Buddhism and Magadhan imperialism, Zoroastrianism and the Achaemenian empire were inseparably intertwined. By the sixth century B.C. the Persians had secured a firm economic base in the fertile valleys of Iran and needed only a capable leader to transform them from mere restless tribes into an imperial community. Such a leader appeared in the person of Cyrus (558-530 B.C.), who overthrew Median rule, crushed Croesus of Lydia in 547, and triumphantly marched into the great city of Babylon in 539. It was under Cyrus that Baluchistan and the districts of Hazara and Peshawar were incorporated into the Achaemenian empire for the first time.

The imperial tradition created by Cyrus was continued by his successors Cambyses (530-522 B.C.) and Darius the Great (522-486 B.C.). Darius made his empire the greatest power of his time, and "India" (the northwest frontier area, Baluchistan and southern Punjab) became one of his richest satrapies, paying an annual tribute in gold valued in current terms as close to some nine million dollars. His armies included numerous Indian levies along with a host of other tribes. It was this standing army, polyglot, mobile, efficient, and mercenary, that formed the backbone of his empire. The emperor kept in close touch with his satrapies through a network of spies, his "eyes and ears," a feature also common to the Maurya imperial system. Darius had his imperial pronouncements engraved on rocks, so that not only his immediate subjects, but also posterity may know the majesty and power of the Great Ruler. As we shall see later, Asoka very widely used the medium of rock- and pillar-engraved inscriptions, closely following the literary style of Darius, to communicate with his people.[10]

Under Xerxes (486-465 B.C.) and his successors the Achaemenian empire began its march to decline and doom. The rebellions of the provinces and wars against the Greeks, mounting expenses of the imperial administration, and the burdens of taxation on the people sapped the vitality of the empire. The structure of Achaemenian imperial rule was gradually so weakened that it needed only a spectacular military defeat to send it reeling to its destruction, and that came when Alexander of Macedon overran the Persian empire in a series of spectacular campaigns beginning in 334 B.C.

The story of Alexander and his brilliant exploits is so well known that it needs only the briefest recapitulation here. Alexander, son of Philip II of Macedon, was born in the summer of 356. For his tutor he had the celebrated philosopher Aristotle (384-322 B.C.), and his keen and curious mind learned the art of war and the intricacies of the science of government as easily as it assimilated the lofty ethical and aesthetic ideas of his famous mentor. Soon after his accession in 336, Alexander embarked upon a career of conquest that was to lead him to the Punjab in India only to return to Babylon and a premature demise in 323 at the age of thirty-three.

In the spring of 334, Alexander crossed the Dardanelles leading an army numbering some thirty thousand foot soldiers and five thousand horse. He also carried with him a group of technicians, experts in operating siege trains, historians and men of letters to write about his story, and botanists and men of scientific inclination to collect information on everything that was new and curious for the Greek genius. By July 331, he had crossed the Euphrates and Tigris rivers and marched on Gaugamela. On the first of October 331, he defeated the Persians in a brilliant battle and by 327 B.C. completed the conquest of eastern Persia and the tracts of Bactria and Bokhara as far as the Jaxartes (Syr Darya). In May 327, he was ready to march into India.

The destruction of the Achaemenian empire was a spectacular feat of arms. But the prospect of an Indian campaign was no less exciting. To the ancient Greeks India was a land of fabulous wealth and innumerable people, of mysterious rivers and bizarre animals, a land that lay farthest east of the inhabited world. Alexander knew that his Indian campaign would be difficult, and he prepared for it methodically. At the outset, he secured the cooperation of two Indian rulers who had their personal grievances against Porus, the most powerful of the Indian kings in north-western India.

The world of northwestern India was then a world of tribes effective in preserving their own independence but incapable of united resistance against a threat from without. In the distant Gangetic lands ruled Dhana Nanda with a vast treasury and a numerous army. But Alexander's march scarcely ruffled his sleep. Alexander conquered one tribe after another, overcoming gallant but tragic resistance. By the spring of 326 B.C. he was in Taxila where he held a grand *durbar* (a meeting of a king with his courtiers) receiving homage from some of the smaller chiefs of the area. Now news came that Porus (whose kingdom lay between the Jhelum and the Chenab rivers) was getting ready for battle. It was not without a sense of annoyance that the Macedonian received this message of defiance from the Indian king. Alexander ordered immediate preparations to prevent his adversary from gathering further strength. The crossing of the Jhelum River was effected with great secrecy, and Alexander was now ready to engage Porus.

Porus had not underestimated his opponent and had mustered a strong force of thirty thousand foot soldiers, four thousand horse and three hundred chariots along with two hundred war elephants. It was the first time that the Greek army was to be confronted by these forbidding pachyderms, and there was some apprehension that the Macedonian horses might shy at their sight and thus cause movements beyond the control of their riders. Porus deployed his army according to the traditional Indian strategy with the elephants in front, the infantry in the rear, and cavalry and chariots on the flanks.

Alexander keenly studied his adversary's battle plan and decided to deliver a surprise attack on the Indian flanks. This caused great confusion among the enemy. The elephants stampeded, and in the melee the Indian army was massacred. They fought bravely and bitterly but lost the day against superior organization and leadership. Porus himself was wounded and lost twenty thousand foot soldiers, three thousand horse, all his chariots, and his two sons. He could fight no more and was taken captive.

Porus was then conducted to Alexander, who gave back to

Porus "his sovereignty over the Indians of his realm, and added also other besides his former territory even greater in extent; thus did he treat as a king a brave man, and from then on found him in all things faithful." [11]

Alexander then went on to conquer the many tribes ruling in the area. He crossed the Chenab and Ravi rivers and finally arrived on the Beas where his troops mutinied. This was in July 326 B.C. The men had marched a long way from home and had fought hard. Possibly they had also heard reports of a formidable army kept in the field by the Nanda king ruling in the Gangetic region. Alexander made a passionate exhortation asking them to bear a little more and accompany him to the ends of the earth, which were believed to be not too distant from where they stood. But his oratory fell on sullen ears, and the Macedonian conquerer decided to return, following the old route back to the Jhelum. Alexander sailed down the Jhelum and the Indus, leaving his Indian and Greek satraps behind to rule over the conquered territories. In September 325, he began his journey to Babylon, where he died in 323 after a memorable life of thirty-two years and eight months, leaving behind him a vast stretch of loosely organized conquests and innumerable legends.

Alexander had come and gone. His march through the northern parts of India had been spectacular. Though his fame endured, his power vanished soon after his retreat. Even when he was in India his satraps were murdered, and no sooner was his back turned than the whole elaborate fabric of the empire he had reared with such strenuous efforts crumbled.

Politically the Greek invasion was like an angry storm that pulls down giant trees and leaves masses of rubble behind. It was a spectacular military adventure in the course of which numerous battles were won but very little territory really conquered. But the other results of his campaign were not insignificant. The immediate political consequence was that Alexander had shattered the power of the numerous petty kingdoms and tribal oligarchies of the Punjab and created a military turbulence and a political weakness that were soon exploited by Chandragupta Maurya.[12]

What were the effects of this Achaemenid-Hellenistic intrusion into Indian history? From the time of Cyrus to that of Darius III, the Persian domination over the northwestern parts of India lasted for well-nigh two hundred years. The Hellenistic rule was much shorter, as it did not exceed four years, though the political and military impact during this short period was intense. Almost from the sixth century B.C. onwards, Gandhara and the neighboring areas sat astride the great trade routes that saw the transport of goods and ideas from one cultural world to another. Under Darius the Great a considerable part of southern Punjab "if not the whole of the central as well as the lower Indus Valley" were included in the Persian empire.[13] Under the Achaemenids this part of India assimilated many elements of that international culture which the Persians had developed through their contacts with Assyria, Egypt, and the Hellenistic world. And it was in this area that the precursors and founders of the Maurya Empire began their initial activities.

During the centuries preceding the rise of the Maurya Empire, then, the whole of northwestern India formed a vital part of the international world that stretched from the Indus to the Mediterranean, and the Mauryas were heirs to the culture of this international world. If the Nanda empire shattered the isolation of mid-India, the West Asian interlude ended the national isolation of the country and placed its culture within the mainstream of cosmopolitanism and internationalism. That was the legacy of Persia and Hellas, of Darius and Alexander. This international world impinged on every aspect of Indian life—political, economic, artistic, and cultural—and enriched it to a deep and significant extent.[14] The Mauryas continued to further this trend, and the Maurya Empire, therefore, assumes significance in a new dimension of Indian history as a part of the history of the ancient international empires.

III

The third, or the dynastic, revolution which led to the founding of the Maurya Empire by Chandragupta Maurya, the grandfather of Asoka, took place in 322 B.C.[15] This was when Chandragupta Maurya slew Dhana Nanda. But the Mauryan revolution was but a part of a long and continuing tradition of political changes occuring in eastern India.

The story may be summarized as follows: The contemporary of the Buddha was Bimbisara (*circa* 545-493 B.C.) who, according to traditional accounts, was placed on the throne of Magadha at the tender age of fifteen by his father. Nothing much is known of

Bimbisara's ancestry though later Buddhist accounts make him a scion of a respected Kshatriya family. It may be that Bimbisara's father was a petty *raja* and handed over the principality to his young son for reasons unknown to us. Bimbisara was the real founder of Magadhan supremacy. It was during his time that the neighboring kingdom of Amga was annexed and Magadha began its march to imperial glory, a march that was to find ultimate fulfilment when the Mauryas set up their own Indian empire. Bimbisara's son and successor, Ajatashatru (*circa* 493-462 B.C.), continued the policy of expansion by his defeat of the oligarchic confederacy of the Licchavis of Vaishali (*circa* 468 B.C.) and his conflict with the kingdom of Koshala ruled over by Prasenajit, another contemporary of the Buddha. Prasenajit is described as a member of a Matanga family that could not have been very high in social status. He had a flower-vendor's daughter for his chief spouse, and his son Vidudabha, born of a slave-girl of the Shakyas, destroyed the tribe to which the Buddha himself belonged. After Vidudabha, Koshala was absorbed by Magadha, which was the undisputed master of eastern India by the turn of the fifth century B.C.

The Bimbisarids were overthrown by the Shishunagas, a dynasty founded by a minister of the last Bimbisarid, Nagadasaka. The Shishunagas were in turn replaced by the Nandas around 368 B.C. The founder of the Nanda dynasty was Mahapadma, who began his career as a court barber and won the throne through romantic intrigue with the chief queen of his master, slew the rival princes, and went on to overthrow a number of old tribal kingdoms.[16] When Alexander invaded India in 327 B.C. Dhana Nanda, a successor of Mahapadma, was the ruler.

The long line of kings from Bimbisara to Dhana Nanda has been held in contempt by the Brahmanical chronicles either as parvenus or parricides and murderers. They certainly represented a new breed of men. None of them could claim any direct relationship with any of the old and respected Vedic tribes. They built up their own power through the new instruments that they had forged, such as standing professional armies, new bureaucracies, and support of new social classes—the merchants and bankers. Their armies had little in common with the traditional armies before their times. The traditional armies were tribal levies; the new armies displayed little or no sense of tribal kinship. The bonds that held these new armies together were those of personal loyalty. They offered opportunities for professional and social progress to hitherto submerged social elements. They were much more efficient than the tribal armies since they used new engines of war and destruction. The kings could find enough money to support these new professional armies because of the expansion of trade and commerce and the financial support of the new merchant capitalists. It was with the help of such new armies that the Magadhan kings established their supremacy through long and ruthless wars.[17]

The expansion of the domains under the control of the new kings required the services of a new kind of bureaucracy. The old tribal societies were served by their own tribal elements elected to bureaucratic functions through the support of tribal kinship. The new bureaucrats were selected and raised to positions of power because they were personally efficient and could be expected to serve their masters with total and personal loyalty. The new and expanding power of Magadha meant a burgeoning of opportunities for a numerous professional bureaucracy, an element that considerably helped in the consolidation of the power of the new kings.

These new kings did not belong to the established prestigious social groups. For them, Brahmanism had very little to offer, though a few of them made special efforts to woo it by patronizing the lavish Brahmanical sacrificial ritual. In the new creeds of Buddhism and Jainism, on the other hand, they could feel at home, since these sects minimized the importance of family and caste heritage and preached the doctrine that the personal qualities of a man formed the only valid index of his worth. Whereas the Brahmanical creed represented an entrenched hierarchy of social and sacerdotal power, the new creeds were struggling to gain adherents and hence could be counted upon not to oppose the new kings in their pursuit of imperial power. Soon after the death of the Buddha his disciples decided to meet in a council to settle upon an authoritative canon for the creed. They were welcomed by Ajatashatru in his capital with the statement: "yours is the authority of the spirit as mine is of power," an utterance which neatly summarizes the new relationships between religion and political power established between the kings and the emergent religions.[18]

The new kingship represented a political revolution of great importance in the history of India. Its power was much more extensive, its arm able to reach much farther away than was ever possible for the old states. Its economic basis was merchant capital, and the personal wealth of the rulers was so vast as to become a subject of legends. The last Nanda king was reputed to be a very rich man, though rather parsimonious by disposition. He maintained an army of twenty thousand cavalry, two hundred thousand infantry, two thousand four-horse chariots, and three hundred war elephants. His empire comprised all of Bihar, parts of Orissa and perhaps western Bengal, Uttar Pradesh and eastern Punjab, tracts of central India, and the Deccan,[19] an area earlier divided into more than a dozen kingdoms. His capital city of Pataliputra was a large metropolitan center and was soon to become one of the greatest cities of the world of antiquity.

In spite of a formidable army and enormous wealth, the rule of the Nandas had become vulnerable at the time when Alexander invaded India. Dhana Nanda, last of the Nandas, was despised both for his lineage and his avariciousness. The air was filled with suspicion and intrigue, and it needed only a spark to set off an explosion that would overturn the dynasty. An irascible Brahmin, burning with a spirit of vengeance, set off that spark.

In his capital city of Pataliputra, Dhana Nanda, according to the stories about the downfall of the Nandas, had called a conference of learned men. This was an ancient custom according to which kings showed their patronage of learning and philosophy by attending conferences and distributing largesses to deserving scholars. At this conference was present a Brahmin named Kautalya, who came from Taxila in the northwest of India. The assembled pundits praised Kautalya's erudition, but his homely appearance was the cause of derisive comments by the king. Angered at the king's facetiousness, Kautalya swore vengeance against the ruling dynasty and fled from the city to elude the royal guards that were commanded to pursue the Brahmin who had dared utter public imprecations against the king. Kautalya then took to forest trails and found a young lad playing at kings and court in a clearing in a wood. He liked the lad, inquired about his family, and discovered that he was an orphan raised by a family of forest folk. This lad was Chandragupta Maurya. The Buddhist books tell us that Chandragupta was born a posthumous son of a small chieftain who was killed in a border war. Chandragupta's mother gave him over to a family living in the forests as she fled for her own safety. There, in the depths of the jungles, Chandragupta was brought up.[20]

In spite of his presumed royal family background, Chandragupta was a plebeian when he was discovered by Kautalya. The young Chandragupta and his mentor Kautalya were made for each other. Kautalya felt that the youth would be an excellent instrument for fulfilling his vow of vengeance against the Nandas. For Chandragupta it was an opportunity of a lifetime. He proved receptive and intelligent and grew into a knowledgeable and practical leader under the tutelage of Kautalya in Taxila. The Greek accounts indicate that Chandragupta was in the Punjab when Alexander's legions thundered into India, and that the future Maurya emperor had a meeting with the Macedonian conqueror. The Greek accounts describe him at this time, in 327-326 B.C., as a mere youth.[21] In that case, we may surmise that Chandragupta was born around 347 B.C., and perhaps in Magadha. If Chandragupta was a witness to the Greek invasion, he seems to have derived two conclusions from his observations. One was that there was excellent warrior material among the tribes of the Punjab, and the second was that the Indian methods of army organization and fighting were antiquated and needed a thorough change. He made skilful use of his conclusions in creating an army for himself to win the throne and to build up an efficient military machine after he became the emperor.

As we have seen, the collapse of the Greek Empire in India began even as Alexander was retreating from the country. As Justin puts it, India "as if the yoke of servitude had been shaken off from its neck, had put his prefects to death." [22] It is possible that this was a spontaneous movement for freedom on the part of the conquered tribes that was ably turned to advantage by Chandragupta to lead his own revolution. The Mauryan revolution, then, began possibly as the year 325 B.C. opened. Chandragupta gathered round him elements from the republican and monarchical tribes and marched on to Magadha. This, the first attempt, seems to have been defeated. Chandragupta then withdrew to the Punjab, regrouped his forces, and began his second attempt. He may have consolidated his hold over the Punjab, gone on to subvert the administration and revenues of some of the provinces of the

Nanda empire, and finally attacked the capital of Pataliputra. The city was stormed and Dhana Nanda put to the sword.

Chandragupta had come a long way since he left his childhood abode in the forests. He was now emperor and successor to the areas included in the Nanda empire. It must have taken Chandragupta a few years to establish his authority over the empire that included areas of Uttar Pradesh, Madhya Pradesh, Maharashtra, and Mysore, besides Bihar and Orissa. To these areas were now added the Punjab, Gujarat, and Saurashtra. In the northwest, he came into conflict with Seleucus Nicator, a general of Alexander, who had made attempts to reassert Greek authority in India sometime during 305-303 B.C. [23] The attempt was foiled and ended with a treaty whereby Chandragupta gave Seleucus five hundred war elephants, and the Greek ceded to the Maurya emperor the two satrapies of Archosia (Kandahar) and Paropanisadae (Kabul) and parts of Aria (Herat) and Gedrosia (Baluchistan). The newly established friendship was further cemented by a matrimonial alliance, and the dispatch of an ambassador named Megasthenes to the court of Pataliputra. Megasthenes lived in Pataliputra from 304 to 300 B.C. and, on the basis of his personal observations, compiled his *Indika*, quotations from which became the source of much of the information on ancient India in the writings of the classical historians.

By 304 B.C. Chandragupta commanded a vast empire that stretched from Kabul and Kandahar in the north to Mysore in the south, and from Saurashtra in the west to parts of Bengal in the east. Raised in penury and obscurity, Chandragupta now lived in splendor and pomp in the magnificent city of Pataliputra. As Megasthenes describes it the city was 9½ miles long and 1½ miles wide. It was located at the confluence of the Son and Ganges rivers and was surrounded by a moat sixty feet deep and two hundred yards wide and fordable by small boats. The moat was filled with the waters of the Son into which was discharged the city sewage. Beyond the moat lay a massive timber palisade protecting the city. The city had sixty-four gates and 570 towers from which archers could rain a shower of arrows in case of an attack. The city was built mainly of wood.

In the heart of the city stood the imperial palace set in a fine park with fountains and fish ponds, a palace more splendid than similar buildings in Susa and Ecbatana. The pillars of the palace were gilded and inside were magnificent thrones, chairs of state, great vessels of gold, silver, and copper studded with precious stones.

The public appearances of the emperor were occasions of pageantry and grandeur. The emperor was carried in a golden litter adorned with strings of pearls hanging on all sides. His linen robe was embroidered in gold and purple, and before him marched attendants carrying silver incense pans. The emperor was followed by armed men, and his immediate bodyguard was composed of armed women.

The emperor's favorite diversion was the hunt in the royal game preserve. Attendants beat the quarry all round into an area overlooked by a platform from which the king discharged arrows. He made short journeys on horseback, but for long expeditions he rode in a chariot drawn by elephants. The palace was open to all comers, and the king spent a large part of his day attending to public affairs and dispensing justice.

Of Chandragupta's family life little is known. We know that he had at least one son, Bindusara, who became his successor. If the traditions of Kautalya are to be believed, Chandragupta must have been a staunch supporter of the Brahmanical religion and performed all the ritualistic ceremonies ordained by it. But the Jain tradition suggests a somewhat different conclusion. We are told that toward the end of his career Chandragupta followed a Jain saint called Bhadrabahu to the south and ended his days by fasting to death according to the Jain custom. Some place names in Mysore preserve echoes of this tradition. If the Jain tradition is correct, then we must assume that Chandragupta abdicated, though there was no valid reason why he should have done so. There is mention of a great famine in the north at this time, but this would hardly induce an energetic leader like Chandragupta to abdicate his responsibilities toward his subjects at a critical moment. The most that can be reasonably inferred is that, like other members of his family, Chandragupta was rather heterodox in his religious views and may have patronized a dissident creed like Jainism as was done by his son and grandson later. His reign lasted for twenty-four years, and his end must have come around 300-299 B.C.

The administration of the vast empire reflected both an imperial vision and political ingenuity. The empire was divided into several provinces, and at least four are known by name. The king was assisted by a council of ministers and commanded a large standing army. Since we will have occasion to discuss Mauryan administration under Asoka at another point, it is not necessary to go into the details here. Suffice it to say that the administration was both benign and efficient. Megasthenes states that crime was rare; this may be true because this was an era of plenty, and the efficient administration of the empire helped to suppress crime. Megasthenes gives almost a lyrical description of Indian life under Chandragupta when he says: "The inhabitants, in like manner, having abundant means of subsistence, exceed in consequence the ordinary stature, and are distinguished by their proud bearing. They are also found to be well-skilled in the arts, as might be expected of men who inhale a pure air and drink the very finest water. And while the soil bears on its surface all kinds of fruits which are known to cultivation, it has also underground numerous veins of all sorts of metals, for it contains much gold and silver, and copper and iron in no small quantity, and even tin and other metals, which are employed in making other articles of use and ornament, as well as the implements and accoutrements of war." [24] This prosperity was reflected in the dress of the people, for the rich citizens dressed gaily "in flowered muslins embroidered with jewels, and an umbrella was carried by an attendant behind the head of a noble when he went into the road." The poorer people wore fillets or turbans and robes of pure white muslin or linen.

The empire was great, and the people were happy. And in prosperity and pageantry Chandragupta lived for twenty-four eventful years. His achievements were remarkable. Brought up an orphan, he became the first and one of the greatest emperors India has ever seen. A great general, an able administrator, and a remarkable personality, Chandragupta stands at the very head of the array of the great rulers of India.

kinds, artificial and natural, for instruction "can render only a docile being conformable to the rules of discipline and not an undocile being. The study of sciences can tame only those who are possessed of such mental faculties as obedience, hearing, grasping, retentive memory, discrimination, inference, and deliberation, but not others devoid of such faculties." [4]

The educational process was divided into two phases, one of which concerned the learning of the three r's, reading and writing an alphabet and arithmetic. This was completed by the age of eight. Then came the more advanced stage involving the learning of all such subjects as would prepare the individual for his vocation in life. The first subject to be taught was the Sanskrit language in which were preserved the sacred books and which was the language of culture. The next subject to be studied was the science of *Anvikshaki,* which comprised the existing philosophical systems, orthodox and heterodox. The inclusion of dissident philosophies in the educational curriculum of a prince was obviously intended to make him aware of the divergent approaches to the problem of human existence and to strengthen his own faith in the Brahmanical religion.

Next came the science of *Varta,* which concerned a comprehension of what is wealth and non-wealth. Agriculture, cattle-breeding, and trade comprised the three principal subjects under this heading. Varta was considered most useful "in that it brings in grains, cattle, gold, forest-produce, and free labor. It is by means of the treasury and the army obtained solely through Varta that the king can hold under his control both his and his enemy's party." [5] This science was taught to the prince by government superintendents familiar with the theoretical as well as practical operations of the economic and fiscal functions of the state.

The last and most important part of the education of a prince came with instruction in *Dandaniti,* or the science of polity. Kautalya gives us this explanation of it: "That sceptre on which the well-being and the progress of the sciences of *Anvikshaki,* the triple Vedas, and Varta depend is known as Danda (punishment), that which treats of Danda is the law of punishment or science of government. It is a means to make acquisitions, to keep them secure, to improve them, and to distribute among the deserved the profits of improvement. It is on this science of government that the course of the progress of the world depends." [6] The science of government meant the philosophy of the state and the ways to implement that philosophy in the actual day-to-day governance of the territory and people of that state. The king was as much concerned with the arts of peace as with the sciences of war, and instruction in both was deemed essential for the education of a prince.

The forenoons were spent in practical instruction in the use of weapons and vehicles of war like the elephants, horses, chariots, knowledge of offensive and defensive tactics, and the use of subversion and diplomacy. The afternoons were spent in listening to lessons of history as preserved in various types of literature, such as chronicles, tales, illustrative stories, aspects of religion and polity. The rest of the day was devoted to new instructions, revision of old lessons, and discussion on and elaboration of parts either not fully comprehended or only superficially grasped. The instructors were teachers of acknowledged authority and repute, professional bureaucrats, and theoretical and practical politicians. For his part the student was expected to live a life of simplicity and purity, devoting himself to disciplining his instincts and thoughts, and learning to act with deliberation, discrimination, and decision.

What was the philosophy underlying such a rigid and elaborate scheme of training a prince? Kautalya advocates three main premises. In the first place, the prince had to be trained to comprehend and solve, efficiently and successfully, the problems of power confronting him at his accession. The science of government, according to Kautalya, is concerned with the problem of power or force, the coercive force of the state. The king must adequately understand the nature of power and use that power in a balanced way. Kautalya says "whoever imposes severe punishment becomes repulsive to the people; while he who awards mild punishment becomes contemptible. But whoever imposes punishment as deserved becomes respectable. For punishment (danda) when awarded due consideration, makes the people devoted to righteousness and to works productive of wealth and enjoyment; while punishment, when ill-awarded under the influence of greed and anger owing to ignorance, excites fury even among hermits and ascetics dwelling in forests, not to speak of householders. But when the law of punishment is kept in abeyance, it gives rise to such disorder as is implied in the proverb of fishes [*matsyanyaya*

—rule of the big fish swallowing the small]." [7] The basis of the state was power, for the state is a punitive as well as protective institution, and the prince could not be well equipped to run this apparatus of power unless he adequately understood the nature of power. The two distinct sources of power were to be found in the state's ability to control corporate economic life and activity and regulate the individual life through patronage to the generally accepted values of life. The state had the right to levy taxes, regulate trade and industry, possess extensive tracts of agricultural and forest land, own mineral resources, and exact tribute. This control over economic activity gave the Mauryan state enormous power.

In the second place, the state was also expected to encourage the individual in his pursuit of certain values of life. It is this aspect of the sources of power that legitimized power itself, for danda (force, coercion or power) could be legitimate only if used in pursuit of *dharma* (justice, ethical well-being). The values commonly accepted as proper aims of individual exertion were *dharma* (duties, morality), *artha* (prosperity), and *kama* (biological and cultural fulfillment).[8] A proper study of these ideals of life as discussed in the sacred works, as well as works of history and mythology, was a prerequisite for any sound training in statecraft. Third, since politics is concerned with power, it could not be a static construct; it is essentially a process that changes with times and situations. Thus, proficiency in politics required not only a sound theoretical background but also, and perhaps more so, a training in the practice of political relations. The king's power made him vulnerable as well as strong. He was vulnerable because there could be a constant and continuous threat to his power either from within his realm or from outside. To meet this challenge, he had to know not only how to rule over his own people, but also to guard himself against the machinations of rival powers and use adequate methods to contain such challenges. His power was a source of strength, but that strength had to be used with wisdom and discrimination so that the king could make new acquisitions, protect those he already possessed, enlarge his holdings, and bring about an equitable distribution of the profits of his efforts.

In the Kautalyan view, then, the king had two objectives in life, one of which was the exercise of power and the other the practice of benevolence. The one tended to create situations of despotism, and the other led to thoughts of transcendence. The king had to strike a balance between the two, and for this a proper education for a prince was a desideratum. In many instances, an adequate and thorough education could alone be the dividing line between despotism and benevolence, acting as a check on the inherent despotic tendencies of the state as a power structure.

III

The education of a prince took from eight to ten years. At the age of eighteen he was ready for practical training in statecraft. Such an opportunity was provided for him in his appointment as a viceroy or governor of a province. We are told that Asoka served as governor at two places. These were Ujjain and Taxila. He spent eleven years at Ujjain. This was an important assignment, for Avanti, of which Ujjain was the capital, was a vital part of the empire because of its central location, agricultural wealth, and commercial importance. Avanti comprised a large part of central India north of the Vindhya Mountains; its heartland in Malwa was famous for its wheat. The province was first annexed to the Magadhan empire during the time of Ajatashatru, the son and successor of Bimbisara. It became a part of the Nanda empire when the Nandas supplanted the Shishunagas and was acquired by Chandragupta when he overthrew the last Nanda king.

The area of central India contained a number of tribes enjoying various degrees of autonomy. Its incorporation into a great empire only temporarily subdued the republican ardor of the tribes in the area, and soon after the decline of the Mauryas, the region once again reverted to rule by oligarchic republics. It is this stubborn republican spirit that must have been a cause of political anxiety for the Mauryas and that may have been a reason for Asoka's appointment as a governor and his long stay there. The conflict between tribe and empire is a persistent factor in the history of ancient India, and the history of central India before and after the Maurya Empire is a good illustration of the continuance of this conflict in different forms.

Avanti had two important centers of Buddhism, Vidisha (modern Bhilsa near Bhopal in Madhya Pradesh) and Kakanadabota (*Sanchi,* where the famous stupa stands). It was while serving as a

governor at Ujjayini that Asoka met a young lady from a merchant family. This lady was called Devi, and Asoka fell in love
with her and married her. Of this union were born a son named
Mahendra and a daughter called Samghamitra, both of whom
became famous in the history of Buddhism as being responsible
for the conversion of Ceylon and the founding of the order of
monks and nuns in that island.

The province over which Asoka ruled as a governor was an
important center of trade and commerce. The great monasteries
of Bhilsa and Samchi were located near important trade routes
connecting cities in Bihar with western India on the one hand,
and south India on the other. The province continued to be Asoka's special concern when he became emperor; we find that he
ordered frequent inspections of its administration to prevent mis-
use of bureaucratic power.

Asoka's second governorship was in the far northwest, in the
province of Gandhara.[9] It comprised the present-day districts of
Peshawar and Rawalpindi in western Pakistan. Its capital was
Taxila (Takshashila), famous as a center of trade and learning in
the annals of early Buddhism. Trade routes from the south and
the east converged on it, and the town was a center for the exchange of goods from the Indian interior, central Asia, Bactria,
and Parthia. In 327 B.C. Ambhi, the king of Taxila, submitted to
Alexander and rendered him invaluable assistance in providing
supplies of grain, equipment, and intelligence for the Greek invasion. As a reward Ambhi was continued as a ruler of Taxila by
Alexander. Under Chandragupta the province became a part of
the Maurya Empire and was governed by a viceroy. An important
highway connected Taxila with the imperial capital Pataliputra;
along this road the Greek envoy, Megasthenes, had traveled to
reach his ambassadorial post. It was some 1,150 miles in length
and was constructed in eight stages. In its course it crossed the
Indus, Jhelum, Beas, Sutlaj, Jamuna, and the Ganges rivers and
connected the important cities of the Punjab with those of Magadha.[10]

Bindusara had appointed his son, Sumana, as governor of Taxila, who was found incapable of keeping the province under adequate control. Asoka, as mentioned earlier, was sent thither to
quell a rebellion.

The provincial administration was composed of the governor,

his council of ministers, the provincial army and the police, and various high ranking officers appointed by the imperial administration. The governor supervised the administration and was responsible for revenue collection and for maintaining law and order in the territory in his care. He executed specific orders from the emperor, who kept in contact with the governors through a system of couriers and agents. The work of governing a province gave the prince an excellent opportunity of coming to know the people and putting into actual practice whatever theory he had learned during his training. It kept the prince fairly busy, and, since these assignments were away from the imperial center, they prevented the princes from indulging in intrigues against the emperor.

IV

Asoka, the prince, was thus preparing himself for the time when he might be called upon to undertake the responsibilities of the imperial office, if and when destiny called him to it. What was his life as a prince like, and what was his mental makeup? We have scarcely any direct evidence of his life as a prince beyond the incidental information given in Section III. We have referred to his marriage with Devi and the children born of this union, presumably when Asoka was a governor of Avanti in central India. As a husband and father, Asoka was obviously fond of his household and spent considerable time looking after the welfare of its members.

Of his habits, we have to infer from what he says in his inscriptions. These refer to his life after accession, though it is reasonable to assume that most of the habits described were formed earlier in his life. He was fond of hunting and enjoyed other outdoor sports like horseback-riding. He enjoyed the royal gardens and took good care of his animals. Asoka also took a keen interest in bird life and seems to have been an amateur ornithologist, as revealed by the long list of birds that he ordered not to be killed in the *Delhi-Topra Pillar Inscription*. He may have also frequented the festive gatherings called *samajas*, which will be described in the next chapter. He kept a rich table and was particularly fond of venison and peacock, which was regarded as a delicacy by the people of the Middle Country.[11] He had gathered considerable administrative and military experience and enjoyed the confidence of his father, who specially sent him to Taxila to suppress a revolt when his brother had failed in that task.

Asoka seems to have had a keen, sensitive, and perceptive mind, which is much in evidence in his later life. He seems to have developed a tendency toward extensive introspection. He was particularly affected by the sight of misery, human or animal, though this characteristic became dominant only as he advanced in years. The religious and intellectual influences in his early life came from his father and mother. It is also possible that Asoka was influenced by what he knew of his grandfather, Chandragupta, and his friend, philosopher, and guide, Kautalya. It should be remembered that Kautalya was deeply learned in the Brahmanical tradition and accepted all its theological and metaphysical postulates. Kautalya regarded the knowledge of Vedic lore as essential for a king since it taught him to discriminate between righteous and unrighteous acts. He advised the king to perform all the customary acts of worship prescribed by the sacred texts. Kautalya also believed in astrology and the operation of mystic and magical forces and recommended the use of appropriate ceremonies by the king to appease, if not to win over, spirits.[12] We know nothing of the religious beliefs of Chandragupta, though it may be reasonable to assume that like his adviser, Kautalya, the emperor was a firm believer in the Brahmanical religion, at least in the early part of his career. Asoka's father, Bindusara, too, may be assumed to have been attached to Brahmanism. A Pali-Buddhist tradition informs us that Bindusara showed extensive hospitality to the Brahmins by frequently feeding a large number of them, and that Asoka followed this practice until his conversion to Buddhism.[13] With all such influences working on his young mind, Asoka must have been favorably disposed towards Brahmanism. But he did not believe in empty and meaningless rituals, and chided women for being addicted to them in one of his inscriptions.[14] Such an attitude is clearly indicative of a critical mind that dared question many of the popular religious beliefs of the times.

In spite of the Brahmanical influences working on Asoka's mind, he became increasingly indifferent to Brahmanism, though he constantly called upon his subjects to continue to treat the Brahmins respectfully.[15] Asoka's heterodox views may have been due in part to the influences of heterodox creeds in his family. As we saw earlier his grandfather, Chandragupta, is reported to have become a Jain and a great devotee of the Jain saint Bhadrabahu. A Pali-Buddhist tradition informs us that Asoka's mother was deeply under the influence of an Ajivika teacher called Janasana.[16] If that was really so, and there is no reason why the tradition should be dismissed out of hand, then besides the Jainistic influence, there was also the influence of the Ajivika sect on the young Asoka. This influence was later expressed in Asoka's patronage to the creed in the construction of the excavated cave residence for members of the sect in the Barabar Hills.

Jainism traces its origin to a hoary antiquity. Its historical founder was Vardhamana Mahavira who, according to the traditional accounts, was the son of King Siddharth of Kundapura or Kundagrama, located in the neighborhood of the city of Vaishali. Vardhamana lived the household life until the age of twenty-eight. He was married to Jasoda and had a daughter named Anojja, who married Jamali. At the age of twenty-eight, Vardhamana left the household life in search of spiritual values, a quest that he carried on for a period of twelve years. For the last thirty years of his life he preached his religious theories and was called *Mahavira,* or the Great Hero, and also the *Tirthamkara,* or the Ford Maker. Like the Buddha he gathered round himself a monastic following and had great success in winning the support of a large segment of Kshatriyas, including several scions of royal families. Mahavira passed away in 477 or 476 B.C.

Jainism does not regard Godhead as very relevant to human affairs and aims at liberation of the soul through renunciation and purity. Its insistence upon non-violence is much more rigorous than that of the Buddhists, and, to a certain extent, Asoka was influenced more by Jainism than Buddhism in his concept of non-violence.[17] Asoka constantly exhorts his subjects to treat with respect and honor the Jain ascetics, and this reverence for Jainism may have been due to Jain influence in the royal family.

The sect of the Ajivikas was founded by a Makkhali Gosala who was for many years a colleague of Mahavira, the founder of Jainism. Like Mahavira, Makkhali also practiced austerities and began to preach his own theories, which caused differences between him and the founder of Jainism. His asceticism was fiercely

uncompromising. He preached, if the Buddhist accounts are ac-
curate, a kind of a determinism that tended to deny the free will
of man, a doctrine which was anathema both to the Buddhists
and Jains. Like the early Buddhists and Jains, the followers of
Makkhali Gosala organized themselves into a monastic community and had considerable following among the lay people. The
most noteworthy example was that of Asoka's mother, who is described as a devotee of the Ajivikas. His mother's faith considerably influenced Asoka, who asked his people to support and honor
the Ajivikas. Asoka, as mentioned earlier, was responsible for the
excavation of cave residences for the Ajivika brethren in the Barabar Hills. Asoka's grandson, Dasharatha, was also favorably in-
clined towards the theory and practice of the Ajivika sect.[18]

The fourth great influence on Asoka's mind was that of Buddhism, which later became his personal faith. Buddhism was
fairly widespread at this time, and it was natural that Asoka
knew something of the life of the founder and his teaching even
before he formally announced his conversion to Buddhism. The
origin and development of Buddhism and its place in the life of
Asoka are discussed in a later chapter.

We have thus an account of the various religions and the other
diverse influences at work on the mind of the young Asoka. They
were intellectually stimulating and created in him an eclectic
temper that persisted even after his enthusiastic response to the
creed of Gautama, the Buddha, to the propagation and practice
of which he devoted the major part of his illustrious imperial
career. This eclecticism was, in a sense, inevitable, both as a matter of family tradition and because of his essentially curious
mind, a mind that seemed to want to know the many different
doctrines and to respect them as aspects of truth.

The young Asoka, thus, spent his time in both active and indulgent ways. He was no austere puritan, frowning upon the
things that help make life pleasant and joyous. But his mind was
alert enough to tell him that material comforts could be no substitute for intellectual adventure. And the call of official duties
helped him save himself from the isolation of contemplation
by making him participate in the business of war and government. He was certainly ambitious, but his ambition was tempered
by a sensitivity that ennobled his passions and an awareness of

the higher values of life. Thus his mind was cast into a mold that was finally to make him a philosopher king. And in this wise did Asoka wait for the time when opportunities would create conditions for him to test his training and put his own ideas into practice.

CHAPTER III

The Scepter

BINDUSARA HAD A LONG REIGN OF ABOUT TWENTY-FIVE YEARS AC-
cording to the *Puranas*, or twenty-seven to twenty-eight years according to the Buddhist tradition. As he grew old, he was prone
to leave the affairs of state to his ministers of state and to his sons,
who were now acquiring considerable experience in administration and war. As noted earlier we know at least two of his sons by
name, of whom Sumana (Susima) was the older and Asoka the
younger. Doubtless he had many other sons of whom tradition
has preserved little information. Sumana was appointed viceroy
of Taxila, where he did not show any particular tact, and he was
subsequently replaced by Asoka, who was called upon to suppress
a rebellion. This may have led to rivalry between the two brothers. As mentioned earlier, Asoka was sent as a viceroy to Ujjayini.
From Ujjayini Asoka proceeded to Taxila, where he soon re-
stored order and pacified the rebellious populace. It is probable
that after the completion of his task Asoka once again returned to
his old post at Ujjayini, where he remained until destiny beck-
oned him to Pataliputra.

The occasion for this was the death of his father Bindusara in
274 or 273 B.C. Since Asoka was not the oldest son, he could not be
the rightful immediate successor. However, if Buddhist tradition
is to be believed, events soon triumphed over custom. Asoka had
a strong partisan at the court in the person of a minister called
Radhagupta,[1] and the prince had already demonstrated his ability to rule. His opponent, on the other hand, had proved himself
to be inept. Buddhist tradition tells us of a war of succession, and
the narrative is rendered rather gory with the inclusion of such
details as Asoka liquidating ninety-nine brothers and wading to
the throne through a sea of fraternal blood. We are also told that
Asoka's formal coronation was delayed for a period of four years.[2]

This was certainly a rather inauspicious start for a career that displayed so much piety as years passed by!

On the face of it, the Buddhist tradition should excite suspicion about its authenticity. Asoka, to the Buddhists, is the greatest royal name in the history of their faith, a king who transformed a promising sect into a prominent religion of the masses of people in India and Asia. It would indeed be wonderful if through his story, faithfully narrated or piously fabricated, it could also be conveyed that Buddhism was responsible for a stupendous transformation in the nature of this "greatest of kings." Buddhist tradition delights in painting Asoka before his conversion as a wicked and sadistic person, capable not only of torturing innocent people,[3] but also of the greatest sin against fraternal ethics, by which he set so much store later in his sermons on stones! But as soon as this fiend's mind is captivated by the gentle Buddhist persuasion, there emerges a veritable saint, wrought through the alchemy of his faith in the Teachings of the Sage of the Shakyas! There is, thus, the strong possibility of Buddhist clerical self-interest interfering with historical certainty. Such tainted tradition, it is argued, cannot be the stuff of sober history.

Now it is true that a progeny of a round one hundred is an obvious statistical hyperbole even for a notoriously polygamous clan and as such may be easily rejected. But what of the insistence of the Buddhist tradition that there was an interval of four years between Asoka's accession and his formal coronation? Is there any good reason why the pious Buddhist monks of Ceylon should fabricate this? It would serve their purpose much better if they could assert that Asoka was so demonic in his strength and power that, in spite of his fratricide on such a mass scale, he could get himself ceremonially crowned, demonstrating effectively that might in some circumstances could rise superior to an outraged public sentiment. But Buddhist tradition invariably asserts that such an interval did exist, and many authorities have seen no reason to reject this.[4] A careful examination of the tradition reveals that, though there is obvious exaggeration in some details, there is no need to reject its core summarily. It appears that there was a disputed succession; that in this dispute Asoka won, both because of his superior qualities and because of the support he received from ministerial partisans; and that it took him some four years to convince himself and his subjects that he was now really the ruler of India. Assuming that Bindusara died in 274 or 273 B.C., Asoka's accession could be placed in 273 or 272 B.C., and his formal coronation in 269 or 268 B.C.

The sequence of events may be reconstructed as follows: at the time of the death of his father, Asoka was away in Ujjayini, a distance of at least five hundred miles. The news of his father's death would normally have taken several weeks to travel to Ujjayini. After this, Asoka would have spent another few weeks in getting ready to journey to Pataliputra, and it would have taken him at least six weeks to reach the imperial capital. This period may have been used by Sumana to set about securing his own succession, in which attempt he may have been frustrated by the minister, Radhagupta. It is not necessary to presume that a stiff battle was fought; it may well be that Sumana, knowing of the opposition to his claim, left the capital, though it is equally plausible to envisage a skirmish between his forces and those of Asoka. We need not believe that Asoka killed his brother or brothers, though at that stage of his mental and spiritual development there was nothing inherently impossible in his disposing of a few of his rivals. Asoka refers to the harems of his brothers and to his sisters living in Pataliputra and elsewhere in some of his inscriptions.[5] This has been pointed out as a direct refutation of the Buddhist claim that he killed his brothers. But it must be remembered that the reference is to his brothers' "inner apartments" (*avarodhana*) and not to his brothers. The reference also comes in an interesting context. Asoka had appointed a special class of officers called the Morality Officers to supervise the moral and religious activities of a variety of people. They were also expected to enter into the inner apartments of his brothers and sisters to ensure that the law of Piety was observed in spirit, if not to the letter. Now it is conceivable that his brothers, if they were living, would find it extremely derogatory to allow officials, however highly placed and nobly motivated they might be, to disturb the tranquillity of their households by officious visitations, and would have resented such brotherly intrusions even from a pious Asoka. But we need not labor the point too much and can concede the possibility of some of his brothers being alive in the year the epigraph was inscribed.

After his accession Asoka's first task was to consolidate his hold over the vast empire bequeathed by his father. A disputed succession would inevitably lead the imperial and provincial officials to take sides, and after accession Asoka must have felt the need for a general administrative shake-up. This meant replacing officials whose loyalty was suspect, and such transfers and changes involved almost a continental area. Presumably Asoka spent as many as four years in accomplishing this before he felt sufficiently secure in his new position to undertake a formal coronation. This came about in the year 269-268 B.C., as already noted.

The ceremony of the coronation of a prince was both picturesque and majestic. The preliminary worship and sacrificial offerings took several days, and the ceremony itself comprised three parts. First the prince had to obtain the formal consent of his ministers and other leaders to conduct the coronation ceremony. This involved the king-designate's visits to their homes with suitable offerings and gifts. Theoretically, these leaders could withhold their consent, but that practice had fallen into disuse centuries ago and was now reduced to a mere convention. Then came the coronation proper. The prince sat on the throne covered with a tiger's skin and was sprinkled with waters brought from the different oceans and rivers of his realm. He then repeated the coronation oath, whereby he vowed to rule his subjects according to the sacred laws and not to oppress them under the influence of his whims and passions. With this the coronation proper was over. The last part was taken up with the customary games, including a chariot race, and in this festivity all the noblemen and leading citizens joined. Very often the new king celebrated his coronation with release of prisoners and commutation of death sentences, a practice Asoka followed through his long reign on the anniversary of his coronation.[6]

II

What was the empire over which Asoka now ruled? It was the creation of Asoka's grandfather, Chandragupta Maurya. He had overthrown the Nandas and secured all the territories over which they ruled, which included practically the whole of the Gangetic basin and at least some parts, if not the whole, of Kalinga.[7] The Nandas are reputed to have overthrown a large number of ancient Kshatriya tribes, and it is probable that their rule also extended over some parts of the Deccan.[8] Chandragupta added to these territories large areas in the north, northwest, and west, and

Asoka's contribution to the territorial enlargement of the empire lay in the reconquest of Kalinga.

The location of Asoka's inscriptions and his references to what he calls "border peoples" help us in getting a somewhat precise idea of the Asokan empire. Among the frontier peoples are included the Yonas (Ionians-Bactrian Greeks), Kambojas, Gandharas, Rashtrikas, Bhojas, Petanikas, Andhras, Pulindas, Cholas, Pandyas, Keralaputra, Satiyaputra, Nabhakas, and Nabhapantis. The Yonas have been equated with a pre-Alexandrine Greek colony on the northwest borders of India, located between the Kabul and Indus rivers. This colony, it is suggested, formed a part of Asoka's empire.[9] The Kambojas were the neighbors of the Yavanas and lived in the area around Rajauri, including the Hazara district of west Pakistan. The center of their power may not have been far from Mansehra.[10] In the same area lived the Gandharas, whose capital was Taxila. The Bhojas have been located either in western India (Thana and Colaba districts of Maharashtra) or in the Vidarbha part of Maharashtra. The Petanikas are believed to have lived in the Aurangabad area of the same state, with the Andhras living in the areas to their east and south. The Cholas lived on the Coromandel coast, the Pandyas in the Madura and Tinevelly districts of the state of Madras, the Satiyaputras in the Tuluva district around Mangalore in the state of Mysore, and Keralaputra has been identified with the kingdom of Malabar proper in the state of Kerala. The Pulindas, Nabhakas, and Nabhapantis have not been satisfactorily identified.[11] Since some of these areas are mentioned as frontier areas, they must not have formed an integral part of the empire, though they cannot be regarded as entirely independent states either. Their rulers had no objection to the Asokan agents and administrators carrying out some religious and charitable works. It seems probable, then, that they formed a special part of the imperial structure. They were, to use a modern term, spheres of influence, though their internal administration was not the concern of the empire. It is quite clear that the extreme southern part of the Indian subcontinent was strictly outside the political limits of the Maurya empire, and these included the territories of the Cholas, Pandyas, Satiyaputra, and Keralaputra. In the north, the empire seems to have included parts of eastern Afghanistan. Towards the end of his career in 305-304 B.C., Chandragupta acquired the four satrapies of Aria, Archosia, Paropanisadae, and a part of Gedrosia from Seleucus Nicator, the Euthydemid. These corresponded to the areas now covered by Herat, Kandahar, and Kabul and parts of Baluchistan. These areas continued to be included in Asoka's empire also, for a Greek-Aramic version of an Asokan inscription was recently discovered in the Kandahar area of Afghanistan.[12] Curiously enough the Gandharas are called "frontier people," though we know that Asoka served a spell as a governor at Taxila, the capital of Gandhara.

It is argued that there were two Gandharas. One was a Mauryan province and the other a semi-independent territory.[13] If this interpretation is correct, then the province must have been ruled by a viceroy who also acted as a kind of a "political agent" (as during the British times) for the semi-independent territory.

In the west the empire included practically the whole of the present states of Gujarat and Maharashtra. Saurashtra was a province of the empire with its administrative headquarters located in the area of the present town of Junagadh. The governor of Saurashtra in the days of Chandragupta was a Pushyagupta, who is described as a member of the Vaishya caste. Asoka's governor was a Greek (Persian?) called Tushaspa, indicating that a number of Greeks, and/or Persians, must have been admitted to the imperial service in Asokan times, if not earlier. It may also mean that, like the British, the Mauryas favored the practice of appointing an "outsider" to the high post of governor, so that he might bring to bear a degree of impartiality in his dealings with the various sections of the population under his jurisdiction.[14] The administrative headquarters of the Maharashtra area may have been at Sopara, near the city of Bombay, where a fragment containing a few words from the Rock Edicts VIII and IX was discovered.

In the east the areas covered by the present states of Bihar and Orissa, and possibly parts of Bengal, were vital parts of the empire. The capital of Pataliputra was located near Patna in Bihar. Orissa was annexed as a result of the Kalinga war, as we will see presently. The Allahabad region of Uttar Pradesh formed an important province with its capital at Kosam, twenty-eight miles southwest of Allahabad. In central India the province of Ujjayini, with its capital at Vidisha, near modern Bhilsa, was another important area. Asoka served as a viceroy at Vidisha, and it was

there that he "married" Devi, the mother of Mahendra and Samghamitra, according to the Pali-Buddhist tradition. The area of
Rajasthan was also a province of the empire, with its capital possibly at Bairat (where two inscriptions were found) in the Jaipur
district.

In the south as many as three versions of Asoka's inscriptions
are found in one district, the Chitaldrug district of northern
Mysore. These versions are at Brahmagiri, Siddapura, and Jatinga-
Ramesvara. In the Raichur district of Andhra Pradesh are found
the Maski, Govimath, and Palikigundu copies. In the Kurnool
district of Andhra Pradesh has been found the Rajula-Mandagiri
copy. Kurnool and Raichur, therefore, must have constituted two
separate administrative units. Kalinga must certainly have been a
separate province, and the emperor was much concerned about
the proper care of the people of the province after the Kalinga
war, as the special Kalinga Edict indicates. Dhauli and Jaugada
in the Puri and Ganjam districts of Orissa were administrative
headquarters, and special rescripts were issued to officers there.

Asoka mentions a number of Greek rulers with whom he had
friendly relations. The tradition of diplomatic relations between
India and the Hellenistic world began with Chandragupta, who
had Megasthenes as the Greek envoy residing at his court. Megasthenes was followed in this post by Daimachus, who represented
the Greek kingdom of Syria (Antiochus I Soter), and it is possible
that the kingdom of Egypt also sent its own envoy, Dionysus, to
the Indian court.[15] Asoka says that he sent his envoys to the courts
of Antiyaka, Turamaya, Antekini, Maga, and Alikasudara. These
kings were Antiochus II Theos of Syria (261-246 B.C.), Ptolemy II
Philadelphus of Egypt (285-247 B.C.), Antigonas Gonatas of Macedonia (276-239 B.C.), Magas of Cyrene (c. 300-250 B.C.), and
either Alexander of Epirus (272-c.255 B.C.) or of Corinth (252-
c.244 B.C.).[16] Asoka was particularly anxious to let these royal contemporaries of his know what he was doing for his own people
and possibly induce them to do likewise. It is probable that dignitaries from Mauryan India spread the knowledge of their king's
faith to the lands where they journeyed though they were not
religious missionaries in the strict sense of the term.

III

The first eight years of Asoka's reign were spent in the tranquillity of family life and in indulgence of customary royal pleasures and pastimes. Of his family we know only a few facts. His old beloved Devi probably continued to live in Vidisha, her birthplace, spending her days in recalling her young love with the man who now sat on the throne of a great empire. A devout Buddhist, she took great pleasure and pride in the spiritual progress of her offspring, Mahendra and Samghamitra, in the heirarchy of the Buddhist Order. Her son Mahendra was ordained a monk when he was twenty years old, and Samghamitra became a nun at the age of eighteen. Devi may have missed being a queen in her own right, but perhaps she felt a certain pride that, even if she was forgotten as the young love of the great Asoka, history would remember her as the mother of those who converted the people of Ceylon to the Law of the Buddha.[17]

Asoka had several wives and concubines who did not enjoy that august status. We know of at least two queens. One was Asandhimitta, also known as Padmavati, who was the mother of Kunala, the subject of a very tragic tale. Kunala was blinded by his stepmother, the object of his father's senile infatuation. His second queen, the alleged malefactor in the blinding of Kunala,[18] was Kuruvaki, also known as Tishyarakshita, the mother of Tishya, or Tivara, whose donation is recorded in the Queen's Edict. Of Asoka's sons four are known to us by name. One was Mahendra (described as his brother in the northern Buddhist tradition), who became a Buddhist monk and went to Ceylon as a missionary. Another was Kunala, who was blinded by his stepmother. A third was Tivara, who may have also joined the Buddhist Order. The fourth was Jaloka, who ruled over Kashmir. Besides these he must have had other sons who were appointed governors and administrators over the provinces of the empire. Only one daughter of his is known to us by name, and she was Samghamitra, who became a Buddhist nun and went to Ceylon to found the Order of Nuns in that island. Asoka had several sisters whose names, unfortunately, we do not know.

Do we have any significant information about the personality of the king before the momentous change in his life came about? He frequently refers to two constellations in his inscriptions,

Tishya and Punarvasu.[19] The former was regarded as the more important by Asoka and has been taken to be his personal zodiacal sign, while the latter pertains to Magadha. Asoka is also described as rather ungainly in personal looks.

To the people at large Asoka was known as the Magadhan King Asoka or by his titles *Devanampriya Priyadarshin* (Beloved of the gods, Of Gracious Mein). This is in sharp contrast with the presumptuous convention of later times when kings, ruling over no more than a hundredth part of the territory governed by the Mauryas, styled themselves by many a grandiloquent title as Great King, King of kings, and so forth. Nor did Asoka claim any element of divinity, either personally or for his office, a practice common a few centuries later. The nearest he came to claiming any divine favor was to call himself "Beloved of the gods," a presumption which was as innocuous as it was charming.

IV

As mentioned above, Asoka had to undertake a reorganization of the administration soon after his accession. He spent a great deal of his time at his administrative duties and looked into many details often left by other monarchs to officers and servants of the state. That he was a vigorous ruler and administrator is clearly borne out by his known statements in many of his inscriptions. He kept himself informed on all matters of statecraft through reporters who had the liberty of approaching the emperor wherever he was if an urgent report had to be sent to him.[20] He also kept himself constantly in touch with the work of the ministerial council. The major part of his working day, thus, was devoted to the affairs of state, supervising the vast bureaucratic machine that operated the levers of power in the Maurya Empire.

Asoka was a diligent and enthusiastic ruler from the very beginning of his career. He understood adequately the implications of power inherent in the vast complex called the Maurya Empire and used it effectively to maintain the integrity of the empire and his place therein. The Mauryan Empire was an edifice built on organized force, served by a numerous bureaucracy engaged in maintaining law and order over hundreds of thousands of subjects and collecting taxes from them by all manner of ingenious devices. His administrative efficiency and interest in government must have been a part of his mental makeup even before the far-reaching changes were brought about in his way of thinking after the war against the people of Kalinga. Through the first eight years of his regal career, therefore, Asoka was becoming a great emperor, endowed with determination, strength, and vision, qualities which make for a memorable career.

As a king Asoka was expected to participate in the great public activities. According to the ancient ideas kings were expected to offer sacrifices to the various deities on their own behalf and on behalf of their subjects. Before his conversion to Buddhism Asoka may have discharged these obligations with as much zest as was customary for his father and grandfather. He banned this activity later and ordered that no animal could be killed for sacrificial purposes in the capital or elsewhere. He also must have participated in the festive gatherings called *samajas*,[21] of which he disapproved later in his career. The term *samaja* generally meant a festive or convivial gathering with or without a religious purpose. At such gatherings there were shows of dancing, singing, instrumental music, recitations of bardic poetry, conjuring tricks, acrobatic and wrestling feats, and generous supplies of food and liquor. High dignitaries were often present, and in the case of some special festivals even the king was expected to visit for some time. Before his conversion Asoka must have seen some of these festivities. He later came to regard them with increasing disapprobation and finally banned them altogether.

There were other forms of diversion customary for a king. Hunting was a great sport for the kings of ancient India, and though moralists frowned upon its excesses, it was recommended as a good way for a king to keep himself in physical trim. Quintus Curtius Rufus tells us that the king's principal exercise "is hunting; amid the vows and songs of his courtesans he shoots the game enclosed within the royal part."[22] Hunting and the chase took place on royal "tours of pleasure," which combined a picnic and an excursion. On occasions chariot and bull races were held, providing great excitement and entertainment for the royal party.

Asoka evidently enjoyed eating good food. In the first Rock Edict Asoka tells us that "formerly in the kitchen of King Priyadarsin, the Beloved of the gods, many (hundred) thousands of lives were daily slaughtered for (making) curries." The number of animals killed for food in the royal kitchen seems to be abnormally large, but it must be remembered that the royal kitchen fed a large number of people and was also responsible for distributing free food to poor citizens as a part of royal charity. After his conversion Asoka stopped this practice, though he could not give up eating meat curries altogether. He says that only three animals were slaughtered for the royal table then, two peacocks and one deer, and that the deer was not killed regularly.

Asoka particularly enjoyed two diversions. As mentioned in the last chapter, one was working in the garden and the other was riding horses. He took great interest in looking after his animals and spent some time in the stables ensuring that his horses were properly looked after by the stable hands. The rest of his free time he spent in his "inner apartments," conversing with the women or relaxing to the sounds and sights of music and dance performed by skilled and professional men and women. He took his royal duties seriously, but he felt that relaxation was an equally important part of his life, and in almost a hedonistic and epicurean way he enjoyed himself in all manner of indulgent activities.

V

Thus the years rolled on. His empire was secure, his administration efficient, and his regime accepted as a well-settled fact by his subjects. In this wise, dividing his time between royal duties and pastimes, Asoka spent the first eight years of his reign. Then something happened in 262-261 that was to change the entire course of his life and make him that for which he is so much celebrated in the history of India.

That something was a war. Now war is a normal business of kings. Kautalya argues in his famous treatise, the *Arthashastra*, that the ends of polity are four in number. Polity, according to him "is a means to make acquisitions, to keep them secure, to improve them, and to distribute among the deserved the profits of improvement." [23] An acquisition of territory cannot be made without war. Peace and war, he further points out, are two aspects of a single policy, and war must be waged whenever a king feels he has at his disposal instruments of force adequate enough to ensure victory. Asoka's grandfather, Chandragupta, had waged wars and perhaps his father Bindusara did also. The Mauryas maintained a large fighting force, and this was certainly not for idle display. Asoka grew up in an environment in which war was not only a fully accepted institution but also recommended as an instrument of polity. If that was so, why should a single war produce such a traumatic experience in his mind? First let us see what he has to say himself.

His mind is laid bare with unusual candor for us in his thirteenth Rock Edict, the famous Kalinga Edict. He says, "When King Devanampriya Priyadarsin had been anointed eight years, [the country of] the Kalingas was conquered by [him]. One hundred and fifty thousand in number were the men who were deported thence, one hundred thousand in number were those who were slain there, and many times as many those who died. After that, now that [the country of] the Kalingas has been taken, Devanampriya [is devoted] to a zealous study of morality, to the love of morality, and to the instruction [of people] in morality. This is the repentance of Devanampriya on account of his conquest of [the country of] the Kalingas. For, this is considered very painful and deplorable by Devanampriya, that while one is conquering an unconquered [country], slaughter, death, and deportation of people [are taking place] there." [24]

Before we discuss the implications of this confession of an agonized soul, let us find out what this war was about and what led to it. Kalinga roughly corresponds to the major parts of the present-day state of Orissa on the eastern coast. It was inhabited by a number of organized tribes, some of whom may have attempted activities of a depredatory character into the Mauryan dominions adjoining them. Then, again, being on the eastern seaboard, Kalinga was vital for the commerce of India with the countries of southeast Asia. Moreover, Kalinga lay between the Godavari and the Mahanadi rivers and was in a position to control the traffic by sea between the south and Bengal, and also the land-borne traffic passing through its territory. There was, thus, sufficient economic reason for the war.

Was the conquest of Kalinga a new acquisition for the Maurya Empire by Asoka? It has been inferred that Kalinga was a part of the Nanda empire, for which there is support from the *Puranas*.[25] If Kalinga was a part of the Nanda empire, and if Chandragupta obtained control over the whole of that empire by his dynastic revolution, he must have also obtained possession of Kalinga. If that was so, then Asoka's war was not a war for a new conquest but rather a rounding off of an old conquest, or else for the suppression of a rebellion by the people of Kalinga. The inscription says that the Kalingas (*kalinga* or *kalingya* in the plural) were conquered (*vijita*) in the ninth year of the emperor's reign. It goes on to describe the destruction caused by that operation and the radically new policy espoused by the emperor after the war in Kalinga. Then follows the rather general statement that when an unconquered country is conquered, slaughter and devastation are caused, which are exceedingly painful to the king. It is possible to take the last statement to refer to Asoka's conquest of Kalinga as a new conquest, which would then raise the question about the status of Kalinga before Asoka. It would be incomprehensible to suppose that Kalinga was a part of the Nanda empire but not a part of its successor, the Maurya Empire. The only way in which this paradox could be solved is to suppose that the Nandas had not conquered the whole of Kalinga, but only a part, and that it was left to Asoka to complete the conquest.

The war was fought with especial ferocity. According to the Kalinga Edict 150,000 people were carried away into captivity as prisoners of war, another 100,000 were slain or wounded, and many times that number died.

On Asoka's computation, then, more than 250,000 of the Kalingans suffered in the war. It may be argued that Kalinga was then inhabited by a tribal population presumably subsisting on food-gathering, that such an economy could not have supported a large population, and the Asokan figures must be understood merely as conventional round figures. On the other hand, it has been pointed out that Kalinga lay on the periphery of Mauryan areas enjoying a higher technological and mercantilistic development,[26] and this must have acted as an impetus to economic growth in Kalinga too. One of the reasons for the war, as pointed out earlier, may have been control of the valuable trade routes passing through Kalinga, and the impact of trade passing through the area must surely have created appropriate changes in the economic life of the people. On this basis we must suppose that Kalinga was not exactly a "wild" country and must have contained quite a few highly populated areas within its territory.

What could have been done with the 150,000 Kalingans who were taken into captivity? Asoka is silent on this point, but a surmise is quite in order. Kautalya in his *Arthashastra*[27] recommends the formation of villages in this fashion: "Either by inducing foreigners to immigrate or by causing the thickly-populated centers of his own kingdom to send forth the excessive population, the king may construct villages either on new sites or on old ruins." It is interesting to note here that the technical term used by Kautalya for immigration is *paradesha apavahanena,* and that Asoka also uses the same term *apavudhe* in his inscription. It is clear, therefore, that Asoka was putting into practice what was recommended by the theoretician of the Maurya Empire. Kautalya further states that these new villages may contain not less than a hundred families of agricultural people of the Shudra caste with forts guarding units of eight hundred such villages. Such settlements could not have tolerated possession of arms by the "immigrating" population, which means that all these new settlements consisted of a class of people almost servile in their status and unarmed to boot! It is possible that Asoka used this method of clearing new areas in the empire by forced immigration and used the captives of the Kalinga war for such a purpose.[28] The Two Separate Kalinga Edicts betray the possibility of a harsh administration, to correct which Asoka suggests several acts on the part of the high officers in the area.

The war was waged and won. But its impact on the mind of Asoka was so great that it became the "great divide" in his career. The sight of the captives effectively quenched his aggressive ambitions; for the maimed ones, his heart bled; and from the dead, a new king was born. Never before in the history of humanity, nor ever afterwards, has a king publicly expressed genuine grief for a deed commonly regarded as the legitimate business of kings. The war of Kalinga was the first and the last war waged by Asoka, and the sword that he sheathed then was never unsheathed again. From that time on, for Asoka the drums sounded only to preach the Law of Piety. The promising warrior had been transformed into a practicing evangelist.

CHAPTER IV

The Pilgrim

LIFE UNDERWENT A VAST TRANSFORMATION FOR ASOKA IN THE eighth year of his reign. Gone were the days of easy indolence and amusing diversions, of rigid efficiency and awesome might. The sound of the drum was no longer to be taken as a signal to war but a clarion call to moral exertion. Asoka's sorrow for his conquest was both deep and genuine. The straggling lines on the weatherbeaten rocks declare "that of all the people that were slain, done to death, or carried away captive in the Kalingas, if the hundredth or the thousandth part were to suffer the same fate, it would now be a matter of regret to" [1] the most powerful monarch sitting on the throne in Pataliputra. Centuries ago the Compassionate Buddha had declared, "If a man were to conquer in battle a thousand times a thousand men, and another conquer one, himself, he indeed is the greatest of conquerors." [2] Almost mockingly the words haunted Asoka; he had proved that he could conquer thousands. But could he conquer himself? He decided that he must answer this question in the affirmative and felt that the best way to do so was to live and govern in the best traditions of the gentle faith preached by the Sage of the Shakyas. Asoka's pilgrimage on the Noble Eightfold Path had begun.

Perhaps this conversion was not as sudden as it would appear. We said earlier that diverse religious influences were at work on Asoka's inquiring mind. His father was a Brahmanist and his mother an adherent of the Ajivika sect. His grandfather gave up imperial glory for the habits of a Jain ascetic toward the end of his life. And his first love, Devi, was a pious and devout Buddhist. Thus the influence of three distinct philosophies was working on his young mind. The Buddhist tradition asserts that for three years Asoka entertained numerous "heretics" and listened to the exposition of their diverse theories. Long before Kalinga, then, Asoka was in search of a world view that would be both intellectually satisfying and morally elevating. Soon after Kalinga he felt he had discovered such a world view.

Who was the person responsible for the formal conversion of Asoka to Buddhism? Asoka does not mention any teacher by name and speaks as if the whole process was entirely personal to him and did not need the instrumentality of someone else to help him along. The Pali books tell us that for some time Asoka was hospitable to the votaries of Brahmanism and holy men of other sects. But he was dissatisfied with their behavior and decided to make up his own mind in the matter of distribution of charity. One day, as he stood at the palace window he saw a young novice called Nigrodha passing by and felt kindly toward him. Nigrodha, we are informed, was the posthumous son of Asoka's elder brother Sumana, who was killed in the struggle for the throne. Asoka had the novice summoned into his presence and heard from him a sermon based on the verses of the first canto of the *Dhammapada* and was converted to the Buddhist faith.[3] The northern Buddhist accounts, however credit the conversion of Asoka to a monk called Upagupta.[4] The whole sequence of legends is so hopelessly mixed up that it is difficult to place credence in them, though it is not improbable that some highly persuasive monk was successful in impressing upon the mind of Asoka the spiritual greatness and moral grandeur of the Doctrine of the Compassionate Buddha.

II

What sort of a religion was Buddhism when Asoka accepted it as his personal faith? Buddhism began its formal career when a person called Gautama got up from his seat under a tree at Bodhagaya in Bihar. This Gautama, the traditional accounts tell us, was a prince, a son of the oligarch Shuddhodana (Pure Rice) who ruled over the principality of Kapilavastu in the sixth century B.C. Gautama was born in the Lumbini grove, not far from his own city, when his mother, Maya, was on her way to her parents' house. Seven days after his birth Gautama's mother died. He was brought up by his aunt and stepmother Mahaprajapati Gautami. The astrologers had predicted that the young prince would either grow into a great emperor or would renounce the world and found a new religion. The fond father Shuddhodana naturally preferred the glory of an empire to the uncertainty of a spiritual quest as a destiny for his son. Hence he had Gautama surrounded with all manner of luxury, ease, and beauty, so that he would not see any unpleasant sight which might turn his mind away from the world. Three palaces were built for his use: one for the summer, another for winter, and the third for the rainy season. In these palaces Gautama spent his days filled with beauty, music, and dance. At a young age he was married to Yashodhara. Soon Gautama was cloyed with the happiness that sprawled all around him and was disturbed and restless. Then, on various occasions, while out on pleasure drives, he saw an old man, a sick man, a dead body, and a recluse—sights he had never seen before. Suddenly he felt that the life he had been living was empty of all meaning. The sight of age, pain, and death stirred in him profound questions concerning the here and hereafter, and he felt that he would never find answers to them within the precincts of a worldly life. Then, when the news was brought to him that a son was born unto him, his resolve became firm. He was almost frightened of the thought that as his son grew up he would be bound by ties of affection that could never be severed and was convinced that before that happened he must leave his home. That very evening as darkness fell upon the earth, Gautama began his journey in search of light. After having a brief glimpse of his newborn son nestling close to his wife reposing in peace in the bejewelled chamber, Gautama left the confines of the town and began his pilgrimage into the wilderness. He exchanged his princely attire for the garb of a homeless religious wanderer. This was his "great journey" (*mahabhinishkramana*),[5] the subject of countless stories and dramatic representations throughout the Buddhist world in the centuries to come. Gautama had left behind him the world of castes and classes, of princes and paupers, of the smiling and the sad. Did he run away from life? To answer "yes" would be to miss the significance of this grand pilgrimage into the wilderness. He had withdrawn from the world to understand its problems better and to find solutions for them in the tranquillity of the primeval forests, away from the din and bustle of men and women with all their passions, desires, and hatreds.

The first task Gautama, as an ascetic, set himself was to understand life and discover what lay beyond it. For this, he was prepared to meet many doctors and hear many an argument. Making an effort in this direction, he studied under two teachers in suc-

cession. They failed to satisfy him, and he turned away from
them. Then he practiced severe austerities for a time. He discovered that mere austerity was useless. Then, still in search of the
Right and in quest of the excellent road to peace beyond com-
pare, he wended his way to the camptownship of Uruvela, where
he sat under the Ashwattha (*Ficus Religiosa*) tree in deep contemplation of deliverance. There he reflected on the causes of the
all-pervading misery which is *Samsara* (round of births and
deaths) and discovered that desire was at the root of it. Ignorance
and craving were the fuel with which the passions set the universe
ablaze, and *Nirvana* was the only escape from this burning house
called the world. Gautama was enlightened and had found Nirvana.

Soon after this event of epoch-making significance, Gautama
embarked upon his career as the Prophet of the New Life. He
went about preaching from place to place for forty-five years, during which time he built up his *Samgha* (monastic organization)
into a religious force unique in many respects. Then, at the age of
eighty, he laid down his tired body between the Twin *Shala* trees
at Kushinara and passed away into Nirvana. As his sorrowing
followers crowded round him, Gautama said to them "Decay is
inherent in all component things; work out your own salvation
with diligence." The year was 486 or 483 B.C. (or 543 B.C. according to a later tradition).[6]

Thus passed away a magnificent figure. His personality, as revealed in the early texts, is that of a man of stately build and
regal mien. He had a rich and resonant voice, and there were
always on his face a luster and glory which come of incomparable
peace. He was ever affable and of an equable temper that was seldom disturbed even by grave provocation. A master of the art of
conversation and repartee, he was a ready storyteller, recounting
amusing and sarcastic tales surcharged with obvious moral
preaching. A fearless critic of priestcraft, he treated the Brah-
manic ritual with contempt, if not pity. Stepping out of a palace,
he became essentially a man of the people, equally comfortable in
a poor shepherd's hut or in the drawing-room of that great
banker of Shravasti, Anathapindika. Wandering from hamlet to
hamlet and city to city, he spoke to the people in their native
tongue and in a manner which they readily understood. Despis-
ing hypocrisy, pitying ignorance, and warning against fruitless

ment stemming from ignorance of the true nature of the Cosmic Reality.[8]

But the Buddha argued that both the ritualistic as well as the metaphysical approaches to the problem of ethics failed to come to grips with life as lived by the common man in all of his every-day preoccupations. He claimed that his own approach was pre-eminently suited to the problem of man, not only in his relations to his immediate environment, but also in the context of his ulti-mate destiny. Buddhism began as a *Kshatriya* revolt against the domination of the priesthood, but by the very laws of its own dynamics grew into a rebellion against social privilege and hier-archy. The Buddha assailed the Brahmanical priesthood and challenged its theological and ritual theories. He threw open the portals of his own order of monks and nuns to Brahmins and Shudras alike and received great support from the merchants, bankers, artisans, farmers, and lowly sections of the people. He also received support from the leading kings of his day, and this ensured that there would be no political obstructions in the path of the spread of his creed. This support from the broad masses as well as the ruling circles meant that the early Buddhist commun-ity was relieved from the worries of finding means of mainte-nance of the monasteries and the material needs of its itinerant fraternities.

IV

Of the doctrines of the Buddha our earliest evidence comes from the Pali books. Buddhism declares that life, as we under-stand and live it, is misery; transcending life is happiness. The Theory of Dependent Origination (*pratitya samutpada*) attempts to explain the phenomenon of existence in terms of cause and effect. Karma (the sum total of the results of our desires and actions), it says, is the bond of life; Karma is born of selfish desire, which, in itself, is the offspring of ignorance. To shed ignorance is to understand the misery of the phenomenal world, the origin of misery, its cessation, and the way leading to cessation. These are the Four Noble Truths. The Path consists of Right Outlook, Right Aims, Right Speech, Right Action, Right Livelihood, Right Effort, Right Mindfulness, and Right Meditation—in short, a training in *Shila, Samadhi,* and *Pradnya* or character, mental faculties, and intellect. Buddhism accepts the doctrines of

Karma and rebirth but holds that there is no warrant for a belief in soul, which is rejected as a relic of primitive animism. Buddhism enthrones reason in the place of revelation and makes man his own maker. If the thoughts are pure and unsullied by selfish desire, ill will, and illusion, and so are speech and actions, the Buddha declares, one need not offer oblations to the gods, nor need one go to the Ganges to wash away one's sins, since a well in the backyard may serve the same purpose.

Gautama was primarily concerned with man, not with men with all their classes and castes, their social hierarchy and economic privileges. Morals, not the accident of a lineage, he asserted, was the norm of a man's worth. As far as he and his monastic organizations were concerned, the caste system was a system of annoying snobbery. Within his Samgha there was a perfect equality of opportunity for spiritual aspiration and achievement. This was a tremendous challenge, as much to the emergent Brahmanism as to the Aryan hierarchy, which was enveloped in a web of taboos and privileges. The social significance of early Buddhism was that it created opportunities for learning and self-culture for the masses of the people.

In the earliest phases of his career as a preacher, the Buddha, it appears, did not intend to found a *religion*. Rather he favored the formation of a sect of the spiritual elite, who would be willing to give up the household life and adopt the calling of homeless wanderers living on the periphery of society and drawing sustenance from it without being part of it. The ideal put forward by the Buddha was that of Nirvana, a complete ceasing to become, which was declared impossible for one who was involved in the cares of the house and the world. Hence it was absolutely imperative for a man to renounce the world if he was to make a serious attempt to find Nirvana. The householder's status was lower, for household life, according to the Buddha, was vexatious. A man, therefore, should leave his son and wife, his mother and father, wealth and possessions behind and wander forth into the loneliness of the spiritual quest.

In this scheme there was hardly a place for the layman. But without lay support Buddhism could not exist, much less spread. In order to feed the monk or nun, there had to be the faithful lay devotee who worked on the farm or in crafts and donated a part of his income for the upkeep of the Buddhist order and its monasteries. Also, claiming universality, the Buddha could not restrict the scope of his discovery to only a section of the people. It was inevitable that sooner than later, Buddhism developed a section of its following consisting of influential laymen and laywomen.

When the layman was accepted as a vital part of the creed, Buddhism became a religion. It was obvious that the layman, as a layman, could not be promised Nirvana, which was reserved for the monk or the nun. But the layman could aspire after a lesser state and that was the state of *devahood* or the status of a god. The Buddha did not recognize divinity as a creative cause, neither did he reject the gods altogether. The Buddha never concerned himself with the problem of the origin of the universe, for he felt that it was enough if a man understood his present predicament and worked his way out of it.[8]

But if the gods were not the creators and regulators of the universe, it did not mean that they did not exist at all. The Buddhist interpretation of gods makes of them exalted beings who owe their condition to merit accumulated by them through innumerable good deeds in past lives, kinds of angels who had a long life and lived in happiness so long as the stock of merit lasted. Men, said the Buddhists, could be reborn as gods and enjoy the benefits and pleasures of a divine status, though this status was necessarily lower than that of a monk, who was assured of his Nirvana. However long their span of life, the gods were born and they died eventually, whereas Nirvana meant the absolute end of all becoming with its round of births and deaths. However, godhood as an ideal was pre-eminently suited to the status of a layman, and it was this ideal that was placed before him. The entry of the gods also meant acceptance of ideas of heaven and hell, and these ideas too were accepted by Buddhism now. Materials for this were at hand and were taken over from the prevailing cosmological and theological ideas. Godhood can be secured through righteous conduct, whereas hell and the status of a monstrous spirit, wandering the earth assailed forever by hunger and thirst, were the wages of sin. Thus was completed the Buddhist "theology," wherein the Buddha occupied the highest status and was surrounded by a host of gods and godlings and had the power to save man from the horrors of hell. This was the new Buddhism, the Buddhism of the laymen and laywomen, and it was also the Buddhism of Asoka.

V

From its very inception Buddhism was a proselytizing creed. The Buddha's message to his followers was "Wander forth, Oh monks, for the benefit of the many, for the happiness of the many, for the welfare, benefit and happiness of gods and men. Preach, Oh monks, this doctrine, which is good in the beginning, good in the middle and good at the end, with its meaning and in its letter and complete holy life. Do not two of you take the same road." [9] Accepting this advice, the monks and nuns wandered along the highways and the forest trails and spread the word of the Buddha everywhere. Even during his lifetime the Buddha's fame had spread to the distant Deccan, and soon after the passing away of the Master, monastic communities began springing up all over northern and western India, supported by the bounty of the lay followers. The inclusion of the laymen led to the formulation of a distinct "Buddhist" code of ethics, which is discussed in a number of sermons by the Buddha himself. The Buddha asked of his followers that they refrain from destroying life wantonly, that they abstain from taking things not given to them, from uttering untruth, from indulging in immoral life, and from drinking intoxicating potions and substances. This was the basic lay morality. On special days, like the eighth, eleventh, or fifteenth of the bright fortnight, the laymen were also advised to undertake special vows like eating once a day, refraining from the use of unguents and perfumes, and spending their time in meditation. They were asked to cultivate virtues like charity, non-violence, compassion, and forbearance. Five occupations were barred to them. These were trade in weapons, trade in human beings, trade in flesh, trade in spirits, and trade in poisons. They were exhorted to earn their wealth by moral means and generously give charity to the monks and nuns and the Order. Indeed, support of the Order of monks and nuns was considered to be the most desired quality in a Buddhist layman. Such charity, born out of reverence for the Buddha, his Doctrine, and his Order, could effectively prevent a man from being overtaken by his karma. Feeding of monks and nuns, building and maintenance of monasteries, came to be emphasized as the proper activities for good laymen.[10]

With the development of Buddhism the Buddhist view of the Buddha also changed. Initially the Buddha was looked upon as a human being of a lofty spiritual status, the Master, the Teacher, and the Pathfinder. After his passing away, the relics of his mortal remains were enshrined in hemispherical mounds of bricks called *stupas*. These stupas, originally only commemorative monuments, gradually became places of worship, and the pious layman was expected to go and worship at the stupa. As we will see later, Asoka enlarged the stupa of a former Buddha called Konagamana or Kanakamuni as a pious act. The Buddhist laymen were also exhorted to go on a pilgrimage to the places sanctified by the four most decisive events in the life of the Master. These were the Lumbini Forest, where the Buddha was born; Bodhagaya, where the Buddha was enlightened and became the Buddha; Sarnath, where the Master preached for the first time and "set in motion the Wheel of the Law"; and Kushinara, where he passed away. Asoka visited all of these places and set up commemorative edifices to mark his pilgrimage.

The development of Buddhism as a religion of the masses of the people of northern and western India was paralleled by another development. This was the splitting up of the faith into numerous sects. Soon after the Buddha's demise, we are told, there was held the first Buddhist Council in Rajagriha, which collected the utterances of the Master and grouped them in various categories. This council also codified the rules of the monastic order. The monastic code was designed to control the behavior and activities of the monks and the nuns in all details concerning dress, food, and relations with the laymen, and contained a code called the *Pratimoksha* aimed at a periodic cleansing of the Order through confessions of infractions of rules of the monastic code. The Buddha had refused to nominate a successor, and he had left quite a few subjects open. It was inevitable that there would be differences of opinion on many points of the monastic code as well as on aspects of the Doctrine. These led to schisms, and eventually Buddhism was split into as many as eighteen different sects. Such schismatic activity was naturally of great concern to the laymen, and, as a layman, Asoka issued an edict threatening dire consequences for those whose acts led to splits within the order.[11]

By the third century B.C. Buddhism had emerged as a powerful religion, followed by hundreds of monks and nuns and thousands of lay devotees. It had its own "pantheon" and ethics, and its own places of pilgrimage and general worship. It was this Buddhism that Asoka's young consort Devi followed, and in which Asoka began to take interest even before the Kalinga war. After the war Asoka became a formal convert, and with his conversion a new life for the emperor began.

VI

The Kalinga war had given a frightening display of the might of the Maurya Empire. Asoka was both fascinated and appalled by it. As an organization of force the empire was unrivaled. Could it also, asked Asoka, be an institution of morality? Its force had overawed millions of men. Would it infuse morality into the life of the nation and bring peace, contentment, and happiness for the millions who lived in the shadow of its throne? To transform the coercive might of an empire into a moral persuasion was an experiment fraught with tremendous possibilities. Asoka was adventurous enough to undertake it. Indeed, he felt if he was ever to atone for the guilt of Kalinga, he must tame force. For that, he must discipline himself ethically and spiritually. He had been a dilettante, but now he must be a man of dedication. He must make up his mind about the path he was going to tread in his quest for righteousness, and he felt that the Path of the Buddha was the most significant pilgrimage that he could embark upon. Intellectual curiosity is powerful, but faith is even mightier. His quest for a world view that he could adopt as his own was almost over, and a new journey was to begin.

Buddhism, therefore, came as a satisfying relief to the agonized conscience of Asoka. But, he tells us, "Two and a half years and somewhat more [have passed] since I am a lay-worshipper. But I had not been very zealous." [12] What was the cause of this lassitude? Probably it was because the emotion of remorse was still too strong and overwhelming to let Asoka do anything positive, except perhaps indulge in a kind of self-pity. He had vaguely seen that he had to accept Buddhism positively if he was ever to save himself. Perhaps this was also the time when the aftermath of the great war had to work itself out. Besides the psychological reaction the war had also created great problems of administration, of settlement of the captives, and rehabilitation of the devastated territories. New officers had to be appointed, and care had to be

taken that the heady wine of victory did not blur the sense of
equity, justice, and fair play of the officers appointed to govern
the vanquished people.

Asoka goes on to tell us that a year had elapsed since he became
filled with a sense of mission. By 258 B.C., then, Asoka began his
new policy. The immediate reason for that seems to be some kind
of a new relationship established by the emperor with the Buddhist Order. The term used by Asoka in this inscription is *Sam-
gham upete,* which has been translated by many scholars as "having entered the Order." [13] Now the question arises: did Asoka
ever become a Buddhist monk? If he did, what happened to his
position as an emperor? He could not be a monk as well as an
emperor simultaneously. But it is not necessary to translate the
terms to actually mean "having entered" the Order. It may
have signalized an era of close cooperation with the Buddhist Order. It may also mean that Asoka undertook to observe not just
the customary five precepts but the first eight of the ten precepts
ordained for monks and nuns as well. The additional three precepts were recommended for laymen on special days, and pious
laymen could undertake them for all time if they wished. I-tsing,
a Chinese traveller of the eighth century A.D., suggests that he had
seen a picture of Asoka dressed in the garb of a Buddhist monk,
but this may refer to the last years of Asoka.[14] Considering the
lapse of nearly nine hundred years between the actual happening
of the event and its report in the travel diary of a Chinese pilgrim, it is difficult to accept the observation of I-tsing without
reservations. It has also been suggested that Asoka lived for some
time in a monastery as a *bhikshugatika* (one on his way to become a monk) and, as such, may have worn the monastic clothing.
But if Asoka had really become a monk, however briefly it may
have been, he would have clearly mentioned the fact by using the
technical Buddhist term current in his days rather than be satisfied with a vague description of one of the most significant acts in
his career. In view of this it is safer to assume that what Asoka
meant was that he approached the Order for spiritual instruction
and began a policy of close collaboration with it.

This change meant many things. It meant, for instance, that
Asoka must order the routine of his life in an entirely new way,
even down to the details of his diversions and food habits. As an
ardent Buddhist, he could not countenance the cruelty, masquer-

ading as sport, in hunting. He promptly gave up the pleasures of
the chase and converted the picnic tour into a pilgrimage in
search of piety. Hunting an animal at bay could be exciting for
other kings but only revolting for Asoka. He found visiting holy
men of all sects and discussing various points of piety with them
much more exciting than stalking a quarry in a forest. And then
he began to turn to a vegetarian diet.

If slaughter of animals for the kitchen appeared undesirable,
offering of animals as sacrificial oblation was downright repug-
nant. He commanded that no animal be slaughtered for sacrificial purposes in the capital and elsewhere. This must have pro-
voked the ire of the Brahmins, but Asoka felt that he had to risk
it if he was to be consistent in implementing his convictions. As
time passed he became more rigorous in his respect for animal life
and issued an order forbidding the killing of a number of birds,
quadrupeds, and fishes on specific days.[15] This could cause inconvenience to those who did not share Asoka's religious and moral
convictions, but, as a despot, though a very benevolent one,
Asoka was not to be deterred. What was ethical for him, he must
have argued, must be ethical for all, for did he not think that "all
men were his children"?

His moral fervor did not stop at banning sacrificial slaughter
and the killing of a variety of animals, birds, and fishes for food
or sport. The emperor looked askance even at festive gatherings
called *samajas*, where dainty food and exhilarating liquor were
consumed, dramatic and other entertaining shows witnessed, and
people generally had a good time. He ordered: "no festival meeting must be held. For King Devanampriya Priyadarshin sees
much evil in festival meetings." The King, in his imperial wisdom, commended other gatherings with a religious or moral purpose, and the people had to be thankful for these small mercies!
This was imposing morality with a vengeance, and the people
must have wondered about the curious transformation in the
character of their king. Or did they think at all?

Life for Asoka had now acquired a new meaning. Though he
continued to wear the regalia of an emperor, his mind was that of
a recluse in search of moral perfection as preached by the
Buddha.

The tenth year of his reign was of decisive importance in the
life of Asoka Maurya. In the newly discovered Aramaic version of

his edicts it is claimed that after a lapse of ten years King Priya-darshin began to realize the true pattern of life.[16] This new awareness demanded of the king that he live up to the commands of his new faith and do everything that a good Buddhist should do. In the tenth year he "approached" the Buddhist Order. It was also during this time that he went on a pilgrimage to worship at the spot where the Buddha was enlightened. He tells us "A [long] time had elapsed since the [former kings], the Beloved of the gods went indeed on pleasure tours. In them there occurred hunting and similar other agreeable [amusements]. King Priya-darshin, the Beloved of the gods, having been consecrated ten years, went out to *Sambodhi*. From that arose this [practice] of *dharma-yatra* [i.e., tour of the Law of Piety]. There in it take place these [things]—visit to ascetics and Brahmins and charity to them, visit to the elders [of the Buddhist Order] and gift of gold to them, visit to the people of the country and instruction of the Law of Piety and questioning [discussion] on the Law of Piety. This pleasure, born of such [acts or means], is great. The lot [or good fortune] of King Priyadarshin, the Beloved of the gods, is different [in this matter]."

It may be found intriguing that Asoka, while on a pilgrimage of the holy places of Buddhism, visited non-Buddhist ascetics and Brahmins. But the explanation, discussed in a later chapter, is not difficult. Asoka, in spite of his fervent adherence to Bud-dhism, never forgot that he was an emperor ruling over his sub-jects, not all of whom were Buddhists. It was his royal duty, therefore, to show reverence to the holy men of other creeds, along with the practice of his own faith. The tour undertaken by Asoka was a combination of a governmental tour and a religious venture, which also involved a Buddhist pilgrimage. It seems that Asoka spent as many as 256 days and nights on this tour, which meant as many as eight months, assuming that all traveling had to come to a standstill during the four months of the rains.[17]

The place selected for this first pilgrimage was a particularly appropriate one. It was located at Bodhagaya, six miles to the south of Gaya in Bihar. According to Yuan Chwang, Asoka had built the first shrine at this site, and though all traces of the shrine have been lost, it is believed that a replica of the shrine is depicted in sculpture of later times.[18] The object of the venera-tion at this spot was the famous Bodhi Tree, under which the

Buddha obtained enlightenment, and a branch of which was taken by his daughter, Samghamitra, to Ceylon.

In the fourteenth year of his reign, or in 255 B.C., Asoka enlarged for the second time a stupa of a former Buddha called Konagamana. The growth of the cult of former Buddhas was a part of the process of the development of Buddhism as a religion. The Buddhist books indicate that Gautama was preceded by as many as six former Buddhas, of whom Konagamana was the fourth. His importance lay in the fact, as it was believed, that he was the first Buddha of this aeon.[19] The cult of the former Buddhas was a part of the Buddhism of the laity and figured greatly in popular Buddhism. To worship stupas dedicated to the Buddhas was interpreted as an act of merit, and by enlarging and worshipping at this stupa Asoka believed he was performing an act of faith and merit.

In the twentieth year of his reign (250 B.C.) the emperor visited Lumbini in the Nepalese Tarai, the place where the Buddha was born. He also erected a pillar here to commemorate both the place and his visit, and he decreed that the village be exempted from all taxes except the customary one-eighth part of the produce because, as he says, "here was born the lord." [20] Asoka also visited Sarnath, where the Buddha first preached, and set up a magnificent pillar surmounted by a capital bearing four lions sitting back to back and the Wheel symbolizing Buddhism. The Wheel is now a part of the national flag of India, while the national seal has adopted the figure of the Lion capital.

As a pious layman, Asoka was expected to take a keen interest in the affairs of the Buddhist Order. He had "approached" the Samgha soon after his formal conversion, and even if it is argued that he did not live in a monastery as a monk wearing the orange garb of the Order, he certainly came very close to feeling that he had an abiding and perhaps paternal interest in it. Close collaboration with the Samgha, according to the current Buddhist practice, meant visiting the monasteries, listening to the sermons, and discussing with the monks the profound doctrines of the faith. In his inscriptions Asoka refers time and time again to his visits to the Elders of the Buddhist Order. Furthermore, a good Buddhist layman was expected to be conversant with the major texts of the Buddhist Scriptures, and Asoka shows that he fulfilled this expectation admirably. In his Calcutta-Bairat Stone Inscription he says: "The Magadha King Priyadarshin, having saluted the *Samgha*, hopes they are both well and comfortable. It is known to you, Sirs, how great is my reverence and faith in the Buddha, the Dharma, [and] the *Samgha*. Whatever, Sirs, has been spoken by the blessed Buddha, all that is quite well spoken. But, Sirs, what would indeed appear to me [to be referred to by the words of the scripture]: thus, the true *Dharma* will be of long duration, that I feel bound to declare." [21] He goes on to detail a list of sermons of the Buddha in which he found particular joy and significance. A perusal of the list gives us the impression that Asoka was conversant with a considerable part of the Buddhist scriptures, as collected and compiled up to his time, and that his receptive mind was struck with some parts that he felt to be of great significance, not only in his own quest, but also for the Samgha and the laity in general.

Asoka is celebrated as the greatest patron of Buddhism. Buddhist tradition naturally dwells fondly on this part of his career and associates with him a vast monumental activity. He is reputed to have built as many as eighty thousand stupas all over the country, and, whatever we may think of this number, there is archaeological evidence to believe that a redistribution of the relics of the Buddha must have been carried out during the time of the emperor, and that he must have built stupas over these relics. The earliest stupa at Samchi in central India is attributed to the time of Asoka, and a stupa at Bodhagaya was also due to the efforts of Asokan piety. The Dharmarajika stupa at Taxila may also have been built by Asoka. Yuan Chwang, the Chinese pilgrim who visited India in the seventh century A.D., mentions a number of monuments erected by Asoka, indicating that down to the time of which the Chinese Buddhist speaks, Asoka's building activities were still remembered and honored.[22] The pillars set up by him and the magnificent capitals surmounting them still survive to tell us of the greatness of the Asokan architectural and sculptural tradition. Buddhist tradition and archaeological evidence join together to proclaim the piety of Asoka immortalized in countless stupas and pillars all over the country.

One of the major duties of a Buddhist layman is to ensure that the Samgha remains united. The laws of the *Vinaya Pitaka*, the Buddhist monastic code, ask laymen to restrain monks who are indulging in schismatic activities, and for this purpose they are even empowered to exercise the right of refusing to support factious monks. It is obvious that the unity of the Samgha was threatened during Asoka's time. As a good layman, and as an emperor, Asoka felt it was his duty to do everything in his power to prevent schisms. To achieve this he used his imperial office and issued stern warnings against schismatic activities. In one of his inscriptions he declared: "The Samgha cannot be divided by any one. But indeed the monk or nun who shall break up the Samgha, should be caused to put on white robes and to reside in non-residence. Thus this edict must be submitted both to the Samgha of monks and to the Samgha of nuns. Thus speaks Devanampriya. Let one copy of this edict remain with you deposited in your office and deposit ye another copy of this very [edict] with the lay-worshippers. These lay-worshippers may come on every fast-day in order to be inspired with confidence in this very edict; and invariably on every fast-day every *Mahamatra* [will] come to the fast-day [service] in order to be inspired with confidence in this very edict and to understand [it]. And as far as your district [extends] dispatch ye [an officer] everywhere according to the letter of this [edict]. In the same way cause [your subordinates] to dispatch [an officer] according to the letter of this [edict] in all the territories [surrounding] forts." [23]

Asoka thus undertook three specific courses to arrest the impending process of schism in the Buddhist Order. First, he let it be known that he, the emperor, viewed with displeasure any attempt that led to disunity, and that he had ordered that a monk or nun guilty of schismatic activities be expelled from the Order (in technical terms made to wear the white clothes, mark of a householder). Second, he enlisted the cooperation of the laymen and laywomen in this task by calling upon them to read this edict on every fast day (one of the days on which special vows are to be observed, and the lay people are expected to repair to the monasteries to listen to sermons). Third, he asked his imperial officers to enforce his orders and thus used his imperial office to ensure the unity of the Samgha.

Was the Buddhist Order one united organization at this time, or was it already split into a number of sects? From the way that Asoka uses the term Samgha, it is implied that he is referring to one united Order rather than a sect. If this is true, then it must be inferred that schism in the Buddhist Order appeared after the time of Asoka. But then what of the persistent Buddhist tradition, and also the balance of literary and doctrinal evidence, indicating the fact that Buddhism was already split in the fourth century B.C.? Perhaps the Buddhist tradition is confused at this point and is mixing up events of earlier times with those that happened later. From the evidence of his inscriptions it seems that Asoka did not know of any sects (or if he knew, preferred not to notice their existence), and, as such, when he spoke to the Samgha, he referred to the "Samgha of the Four Quarters" (*Chatuddisa Bhikkhu Samgha*) and not the Samgha of any particular sect.

Associated with the problem of the schism is the account of the third Buddhist council as narrated in the Pali works. The Pali chronicles and other texts tell us that the first council was held at Rajagriha soon after the passing away of the Buddha. The immediate cause for this was an irreverent remark about the passing away of the Buddha made by some monks, and the major task of the council was the compilation of the teachings of the Buddha in an authentic form. It is true that the account is full of difficulties, but there is nothing unnatural in the leading disciples of the Buddha coming together to prepare an authentic corpus of the teachings of the Master so as to prevent unauthorized interpolations and insertions.

The second Buddhist council was held at Vaishali a hundred and fifty years after the demise of the Buddha. The provocation for this came when the Vajjian monks promulgated the "ten points" that ran counter to the tenets of monastic discipline. At this council, it is argued, Buddhism was split into several groups that later developed into sects. The story of this council is also full of difficulties, though the fact of such a council has been accepted by many authorities.

The third council, the Pali accounts claim, was held during the seventeenth year of Asoka's reign. It seems that the generosity shown to the Buddhist Order induced many "heretics" to infiltrate the Order, whereby the Samgha was polluted. Asoka ordered a minister to purge the Order, and he did it so well that it resulted in the slaughter of many monks. This caused remorse to the king. Then Moggaliputta Tissa convened and presided over the council that purified the Order. At the end of the council the president composed a treatise called "Points of Controversy"

(*Kathavatthu*) and dispatched a number of missions to various parts of the country and outside. The account of this council is full of difficulties, and on this ground the council has either been rejected as a historical fact or relegated to the status of a sectarian council held after Asoka's time.[24]

The inscriptional and literary evidence thus seem to be at variance. Asoka mentions neither sects nor the third council. If such an important event as a general Buddhist council was held during his time, he would have certainly mentioned it in his inscriptions. The Schism Edict betrays an anxiety about an impending split, and perhaps it is possible to argue that though there existed differences of interpretation on doctrinal points, the *monastic* unity of Buddhism was, as yet, intact. After Asoka, the divergence also applied to interpretation of rules of monastic discipline, and this brought the sects out into the open. Asoka, as a pious Buddhist, felt he could avert the schism but obviously failed in ensuring the unity of the Buddhist Samgha, which he fondly believed would prevail "as long as [my] sons and great-grandsons [shall reign] and so long as the moon and the sun [shall shine]."

The story on the missions is of a different genre. There were, it seems, two sets of missions. One was sent by Asoka to some Greek potentates as well as to territories bordering on his empire. He mentions by name five kings: Antiochus II Theos of Syria (261-246 B.C.), Ptolemy II Philadelphus of Egypt (285-247 B.C.), Antigonus Gonatas of Macedonia (278-239 B.C.), Magus of Cyrene (West of Egypt, 300-258 B.C.), and Alexander of Epirus (272-258 B.C.) or of Corinth (252-244 B.C.). The other group of missions was sent to the Cholas, Cheras and Pandyas, to the Yonas, Kambojas, Nabhakas, Nabhitis, Bhojas, Pitinikas, Andhras, and Palidas. We will discuss the identification of these names and places later on. It is probable that these were missions of good will and information about what Asoka was doing for his people and may not have had any specific ecclesiastical intent. But there is no reason to dismiss this claim of Asokan missions as mere "royal rhodomontade" [25] as has been done by some scholars. Asoka had undertaken a series of tasks aimed at public welfare and morality, and he felt these were important enough to be publicized among his near and distant contemporaries. It is also possible that, along with their political aims, the missions may have spread knowledge of the emperor's faith in the lands they visited, for it is well-recog-

nized now that knowledge of Buddhism had certainly spread into
Afghanistan, Persia, and beyond during the time of Asoka and
before the advent of Christianity.

The missions sent by the Buddhist Samgha were strictly of a
religious nature. The Pali chronicle *Mahavamsa* tells us that missions were sent to Kashmir and beyond, to the Andhra country, to
Mysore and Maharashtra, to the Himalayan territories and Ceylon, and possibly to areas in Burma or Malaya. Epigraphic evidence corroborates to a great extent the claim made by the Buddhist chronicles, and we saw how Asoka's own son and daughter
—Mahendra and Samghamitra—went as missionaries to Ceylon.

The two efforts converged on a single objective, and Buddhism
now emerged as a religion of the masses of the people of the
Mauryan Empire and beyond. It burst outside of the confines of
the scattered areas to which it had spread, and Buddhist communities sprang up virtually all over India. It was no longer a dissident view of life but a system that enjoyed the patronage of the
mightiest monarch of the times. The impetus given to Buddhism
by Asoka was destined to carry it in later ages across mighty
mountains and restless seas to the very boundaries of the conti-
nent of Asia and make it rank as one of the major religions of the
world.

But we must keep our perspective straight. Asoka undoubtedly
rendered magnificent services to Buddhism. It seems that Asoka
was as useful to Buddhism as was Buddhism beneficent to Asoka.
It must be remembered that even though Asoka renounced war,
he did not disband his mighty army, and the fact that there were
no rebellions, at least none that we know of, in his career after
Kalinga, is a proof of the power of deterrence his army had. He
could say that he had shown many a favor to bipeds and quadrupeds (animals), and to birds and aquatic animals, even unto the
boon of (their) life, but for those who were sentenced to death he
could only offer a grace of three days! [26] But perhaps it is unfair
to berate Asoka for not doing something he never set out to do.
The fact that he renounced war as an instrument of his state
policy was a great achievement in itself. For, though Buddhism
preached non-violence, the Buddha seldom interfered with kings
in their warlike pursuits except to enter a protest against them.
From its very inception Buddhism realistically recognized the two
spheres of human life and called upon its followers to render

unto Caesar what is Caesar's and unto the Dharma what belonged to it. The Buddha says: one is the path of worldly gain and another that leads to Nirvana. The Buddha lived at a time when wars were fought all around, and the tribal oligarchies were being pulverized to make materials out of which the monarchies could grow into empires. His own contemporaries like Bimbisara, and his son and successor, Ajatashatru, Pasenadi of Kosala, and Udayana of the Vatsas, fought wars for territory, personal glory, and affairs of the heart. His own tribe of the Shakyas was almost destroyed by a war waged by Vidudabha. The Buddha knew that he had no power over the kings except that of moral force; and when kingdoms were at stake, moral force was something much less than completely successful. As far as he was concerned, the Buddha ensured that his own followers, the monks and nuns, remained as far away from violence and war as was humanly possible. He forbade the ordination of soldiers into his fraternity and condemned the recounting of tales of war and conquest as a mere waste of time for those in the quest of Nirvana. As for the lay world he hoped that the futility of violence would be realized by it and that some day all swords would be beaten into ploughshares. Like other prophets the Buddha proposed, but it was up to the Caesars to dispose, and they willed otherwise. Indeed, it happened that wars were fought in the name of the teachings of the Buddha; witness the invasion of Thaton by the Burmese King Anawrahta in 1057 A.D. because his request for a set of the Buddhist Scriptures was rejected by Pagan! This has a parallel in the Christian Crusades. It is to the credit of Asoka that even when he had the means of leading successful crusades, he believed in spreading the Dharma through persuasion and personal example. The gentle influence of Buddhism left a deep impression on his mind, and once he made his decision to tread the narrow path, he did his best to be true to his faith.

As the years rolled by Asoka became more and more devoted to the cause of his Dharma. The last year mentioned in his inscription is the twenty-sixth year, that is, 244 B.C. He is assigned a reign of thirty-six (*Puranas*) or thirty-seven years (Ceylonese sources), which would mean that the end of his illustrious career came about in 234-233 B.C. Of his life during the last decade we have nothing more than a mass of legends to go by. These legends tell us that the last years of Asoka were clouded with opposition to his extravagant charity, which almost threatened the prosperity of the empire. His ministers, it seems, were obliged to restrain him, and a touching story is told that makes us believe that this mighty monarch had nothing more to give to the Buddhist Order than a fruit, which he promptly gifted away. There are also the tragic tales of the blinding of his son Kunala due to the machinations of his second queen. It seems probable that his second spouse was not quite a happy choice for the emperor, and that his excessive enthusiasm in the cause of religion may have led to some dissatisfaction among his relatives and officers. But all this is a matter of legends that, though touching, can scarcely be accepted as sober history. As we take leave of Asoka in the year 244 B.C. his mind is crowded with thoughts of the unity of the Buddhist Order, the spread of his Dharma, his welfare activities, and his feeling of tenderness for his subjects and living beings everywhere.

CHAPTER V

"All Men Are My Children"

WITH THE ACCEPTANCE OF BUDDHISM AS HIS GUIDE IN LIFE THE imperious Maurya became the pious Asoka. But mere piety was not enough. Asoka was no common person but an emperor of a mighty land presiding over the destinies of millions of men. He had secured martial glory but felt that his new conquest would be less than full if he could not transform his empire of force into a kingdom of righteousness, here and now. Such an ambition needed an administration inspired with new ideals. It had to be adequate and effective, not only in preserving the order and security of his dominions, but also in implementing his ideas of righteousness.

Now Asoka was familiar with the concepts and institutions of empire before his time.[1] During his sojourn in the northwest he must have come to know the traditions of the great Achaemenid and Hellenistic empires that had preceded the rise of his own dynasty. These traditions were "Indianized" by his grandfather, Chandragupta Maurya, and his putative mentor, Kautalya. His father, Bindusara, had continued this "Indianized" tradition of a great "universal" empire and had bequeathed to him not only the concept of such an empire, but also the administrative instrument that held it together. But so far, Asoka must have felt, the empire had existed as a political institution, whether in the Achaemenid-Hellenistic way, or in the "Indianized" tradition as established by Chandragupta and Kautalya. The need of the age was to transform the empire into a human institution answering human needs and fulfilling the highest human aspirations if that empire was to be truly "universal." For this, it was imperative to develop a new order of relationships between the government and the governed. In such a relationship power had to be humanized; this, for Asoka, meant the establishment of a firm and decisive relationship between power and human morality. He was conversant with all the theorizing that had preceded him. It told him that a good king must endeavor to preserve the social order, the order of the castes, and the four stages of life. This was the duty of the scepter, for it is only when power is used with discretion that people behave themselves and create the wealth so necessary for enjoyment in this world. The use of coercive authority was regarded by the traditional thinkers as the king's distinctive function, for force alone made property secure, disciplined the undisciplined, and protected the virtuous from the predatory ambitions of the wicked. It was for this, argued the *Mahabharata,* that the Creator had prescribed the use of institutionalized force which is the state.[2] But Asoka had realized that mere force was not enough, and that it tended to destroy the integrity of one who used it, even though it was for a legitimate end like the preservation of sovereignty. Force had helped the empire maintain its position of supremacy and had taught a group of backward tribes to submit to the authority of a mighty state. But this victory was enervating. Kalinga had shown that even when danda (force, coercive authority of the state) was used for the ends of what was traditionally understood as dharma (right, duty, integrity), it corroded the most vital part of dharma itself, namely, conscience. Earlier speculation had dwelt on the dichotomy of danda and dharma and had pointed out that the success of statecraft lay in using danda for dharma to balance one against the other. But such a balancing feat became unbearable for a sensitive conscience. Asoka set out to discover new premises for his own philosophy of the state.

One of his inscriptions helps us to understand this new state of his mind. Paradoxically this epigraph was issued for the governance of those very people who were the victims of Asoka's imperial wrath, the people of Kalinga. Asoka says to his officers: "All men are my children. As on behalf of [my own] children I desire that they may be provided with complete welfare and happiness in this world and in the other world, the same I desire on behalf of [all] men." Asoka felt that the people must be made to feel that the king was to them even as a father; he loved them even as he loved himself; they were to the king even as his children.[3] The officers of the state were to think of themselves not as masters but as a "skilful nurse" to whose care a thoughtful man makes over his child in the belief that the child will be well looked after. All this may be easily dismissed as pious musings of a sorrowing king, but it was also the expression of a new resolve. The king was to play the role of a *pater familias,* presiding over a large and numerous family filled with a plurality of peoples and societies. His empire was a "debt" for him, a heavy debt that had to be conscientiously discharged. There was nothing revolutionary in such thoughts, for had not Kautalya declared that "in the happiness of his subjects lies the king's happiness; in their welfare his welfare"? [4] But there were three important points of difference between the ancient exhortations and the new policy of Asoka. First, though Asoka showed great respect for Brahmins as religious and learned men, he does not seem to have followed the sociological demands of Brahmanism. In this his intents and actions signified a revolt against sacerdotalism. Sacerdotalism, as a religio-social system, had been in the process of development since the time of the Buddha. As early as the sixth century B.C. a section of the Brahmin group was becoming wealthy and powerful through the performance of varied ritual and religious duties for the community and the state. The institution of sacrifice, which was primarily thought of as an instrument of spiritual welfare, was becoming a means for the enrichment of this group. The Buddha insisted on a distinction being made between the Brahmins and *Brahmabandhus.*[5] The former were pursuing the ideals of morality, devotion, and non-possession and in this respect could be spoken of together with the non-Brahmanical ascetics called the *Shramanas.* The latter were professional priests who enriched themselves with worldly goods by ministering to the religious beliefs and superstitious credulity of the rulers and their subjects. Alongside this sociological development there were the growing demands for extraordinary privileges for the Brahmin group as a whole. For a considerable time, from the sixth to the second centuries B.C., both the state and the community had resisted these demands. Kautalya does not regard the person of the Brahmin as sacrosanct under all circumstances, for he prescribes the punishment of death by drowning to a Brahmin if he is guilty of high treason.[6] When Asoka speaks of respect for Brahmins, he invariably links them with the Shramanas. But his dictum of equality in procedure and punishment applies as much to the

Brahmabandhus as the Shudras. Such an attitude is the general Buddhist attitude and is a continuation of the struggle against sacerdotalism which the Buddha had initiated.

Second, Asoka favored freedom for all sects, whereas in the earlier political theory such freedom was construed as weakening the power of the state. There was also another point of departure for Asoka. This was in the criteria for judging the legitimacy of the adoption of the ascetical mode of life by the subjects. Kautalya allows only those who are past their prime to become ascetics and then only after the proper disposal of the property of their acquisition. Any person who converts a woman is to be punished; and ascetics are not to be allowed free and unfettered access to the villages of the kingdom.[7] Such an attitude is clearly anti-ascetical and contrasts sharply with the attitude of Asoka. In the Rock Edict VII, Asoka declares that ascetics of all sects may dwell wherever they like, for all of them strove to acquire self-restraint and purification. This reference to "all sects" is more a political than a religious pronouncement. Unlike Kautalya, Asoka welcomes the ascetics of all sects, for he is not apprehensive of the effect of their propaganda on the populace in general as Kautalya seems to be. Kautalya was worried about interruption in productive economic activity by the people as a result of the ascetical intrusion; Asoka reached precisely an opposite conclusion in his feeling that the influence of the ascetics would be beneficial for maintaining the peace of the realm and elevating the moral temper of the populace.

Finally, Asoka was convinced that, to be glorious, an empire must necessarily rest on the foundations of love and morality and not *danda*. He was frequently apprehensive about the excessive and arbitrary abuse of force by his officers and exhorted them to be just, kind, and sympathetic toward their charges rather than imperious in the discharge of their political duties. Force may render the subjects submissive and apathetic, but only sympathy and love would induce them to feel a spontaneous affection for the ruler and their state. Asoka was not after mere submission; he valued much more the loyalty that subjects may have for their sovereign if they regard him with trust rather than fear. He wanted this loyalty, for he felt that it was only on the basis of such a loyalty that an empire could survive and be "universal." The implementation of this policy needed far-reaching administrative changes, affecting both its formal structure and its spirit, and to this task Asoka now turned.

II

Over his vast empire, stretching from Kabul in the north to Mysore in the south and from Saurashtra in the west to Bengal in the east, Asoka ruled from his capital in Pataliputra. This city was founded in the days of the Buddha by Ajatashatru, the son of Bimbisara. It was the capital of the Nandas, and the dynastic revolution carried out by Chandragupta came to its climax there, when Chandragupta assassinated the Nanda ruler. We have already referred to the description of the city and its surroundings as given by Megasthenes. Asoka, reports Yuan Chang, the Chinese Buddhist pilgrim who visited India in the seventh century A.D., built in the city many edifices, including a palace and a stupa so exquisite that the pilgrim believed it was built by genii and not human beings.[8]

The center of activities in the capital was the palace. Here lived the king and his wives and children, and in the majestic halls the court was assembled and justice dispensed. The palace, though well guarded, was easily accessible to all callers. Before the traumatic experience of the Kalinga war Asoka spent many a pleasure-filled hour within the precincts of the palace. But after his conversion to Buddhism the king spent the day in one long round of public activity. The king was kept continually informed of what was going on in the empire by the many reporters and agents who collected information. Asoka, says "In times past neither the disposal of affairs nor the submission of reports at any time did exist before. But I have made the following [arrangement]. Reporters are posted everywhere, [with instructions] to report to me the affairs of the people at any time, while I am eating, in the harem, in the inner apartment, even at the cowpen, in the palanquin, and in the parks. And everywhere I am disposing of the affairs of the people. And if in the council [of *Mahamatras*] a dispute arises, or an amendment is moved, in connexion with any donation or proclamation which I myself am ordering verbally, or [in connexion with] an emergent matter which has been delegated to the *Mahamatras,* it must be reported to me immediately, anywhere, [and] at any time. Thus I have ordered. For I am never content in exerting myself and in dispatching business. For I consider it my duty [to promote] the welfare of all men. But the root of that [is] this, [viz.] exertion and the dispatch of business. For no duty is more important than [promoting] the welfare of all men. And whatever effort I am making, [is made] in order that I may discharge the debt [which I owe] to living beings, [that] I may make them happy in this [world], and [that] they may attain heaven in the other [world]." 9

Here we are given a picture of the king at work. What kind of a day was his normal working day? Asoka's inscriptions give us some glimpses of his thoughts and activities, but a detailed account comes from the *Arthashastra* of Kautalya. Kautalya divides the king's day and night into sixteen equal parts of one and one-half hours each. The king rose very early in the morning to the sound of music, and thought over the work of the day. He also performed his religious duties, assisted by the royal priest; and interviewed the physician, the kitchen officials, and the astrologers. From 6:00 A.M. to 9:00 A.M. he gave audience in the Hall of Audience, where he received reports on military and financial matters and attended to the affairs of the people. Then he spent some time in his bath and at the dining table and also studied the religious texts. After a late breakfast he again busied himself with governmental affairs, carried out consultations with the council of ministers, and received reports from the agents. He rested for a short period in the afternoon. He then began his work with the army chiefs and held interviews with secret agents. After the evening meal he was entertained with dance and music, after which he slept, only to wake up early and begin the round all over again.10

The king's normal recreation consisted of listening to music, watching the performance of dancers, hunting, and watching animal races and fights. Asoka tells us that in times past kings went out on tours of pleasure, which involved hunting and other similar amusements. But he changed all this in the tenth year of his reign when he began to undertake the "tours of piety" during the course of which he visited the ascetics, Brahmins, and holy men of diverse orders and distributed charity.

Asoka was a great traveler. He undertook tours of inspection and pilgrimages, and he informs us that in his ninth regnal year he spent as many as 256 nights on tour. This was his famous tour of piety, and it must have also been utilized for making personal observations of parts of the country over which he ruled and the conditions of his subjects. Asoka was particularly apprehensive about the abuse of power by his officials and recommended five yearly tours of inspection, with the frequency of such tours being fixed at one every three years in certain areas.[11] The possibility of arbitrary use of authority was particularly acute in the rural areas, and Asoka expresses frequent concern for the welfare of these areas.

The strength and efficiency of the imperial administration largely depended upon the personality of the king. He not only provided the inspiration for his officers but also kept a close watch on their actions. He was the commander-in-chief of his armed forces as well as the supreme judge in the realm. He was the pivot of his administration, though he accepted Kautalya's exhortation that "sovereignty is possible only with assistance. A single wheel can never move." [12]

The council of ministers thus was an institution next in importance only to the king. The king selected his ministers with great care. There is a reference to the king's council in the sixth Rock Edict indicating the procedure of deliberations and the arrival at a consensus. The institution of the ministerial council existed from very ancient times and was regarded as the most important part of the royal administration. The council consisted of as many as eight members, though Kautalya recommends no more than three or four as being necessary and safe for security. He also gives a long list of qualities to be found in a person before he is appointed a member of the cabinet. He should be a native of the country, belong to a good family, possessed of self-control, well-versed in arts and crafts, and learned in the religious and secular literature, especially the science of polity. He should have an excellent memory, be skilful in speech, possess enthusiasm and energy, patience and perseverance; he should be sound in health and steadfast in loyalty, capable of resolution and ready for compromise whenever profitable and necessary. Of these the most indispensable qualities were wisdom, discretion, absolute loyalty, and an awareness of the necessity of tendering truthful advice fearlessly.

We know nothing about the persons who were Asoka's ministers. The northern Buddhist tradition avers that Bindusara's minister Radhagupta helped Asoka in his struggle for the throne.

If the story has any substance, it may be presumed that Radha-gupta continued to be Asoka's minister. It is possible that some of these ministers could have become powerful enough to control the king. But it does not seem likely that a personality like that of Asoka could suffer such bureaucratic tyranny willingly. The northern Buddhist tradition has stories that Asoka, in his last years, became so extravagant in his charity that his ministers virtually had to put him under restraint. Such stories, however, are clearly motivated, and little credence can be put in them.[13]

The functions of the council of ministers were both advisory and executive. The king consulted it on all important matters like war and peace and the marshaling of resources for the efficient conduct of the state at all times. These consultations were expected to serve five distinct purposes. The first concerned the defense of the realm, which also involved considerations of relations with neighboring powers. Second, considerations of resources of materials and manpower within the kingdom; third, consideration of time and place for action; fourth, preparation against unexpected calamities; and fifth, general administrative supervision. The manual of Kautalya is so concerned with war that considerations of war and peace form a major part of his administrative philosophy. Since Asoka is known to have abjured war after the war of Kalinga, his deliberations must have been concerned more with matters of internal administration than with war.

III

What was Asoka's ideal of kingship? A comparison of his ideas on the subject as indicated in his inscription with the description of an ideal king given in the Buddhist books reveals the Buddhistic influence on Asokan thought. Asoka's approach to statecraft was based on the primacy of *dharma* over *danda,* and in this he specifically seems to adopt the Buddhist philosophy of the state. Asoka was a humanist and was concerned with the welfare of his subjects almost to the exclusion of any serious consideration of royal glory and its enhancement through war, annexations, and unlimited sovereignty. His ideal was the Righteous Ruler (*dhammiko dhammaraja*) of the Buddhist works. The ideal Buddhist king rules without the use of *danda,* or force, and in his hands the state ceases to be an instrument designed to uphold the order of the castes and sacerdotal privileges. The major principles to which this state is devoted are the promotion of virtue, compassion, justice, and equity. The symbol of this state is the Wheel (*chakra*) and not the Rod (*danda*), and the ideal king is the temporal counterpart of the *Bodhisattva* in the spiritual realm. It is distinctly stated in the Buddhist books that the only two possibilities of development for a Bodhisattva (Future Buddha) are that either he lives the worldly life and becomes the Righteous Ruler or renounces the world and becomes the Buddha.[14] A statecraft based on the normal use of force, as envisaged by Kautalya, is generically different from the administrative philosophy of Asoka, which is based on the assumption that human nature is basically good, and that human beings can be made to grow into righteousness by winning their trust and confidence through persuasion, not by coercion.

As Asoka saw it, a good administration must be concerned as much with the worldly welfare of subjects as with their otherworldly good. Asoka constantly emphasized his aim of securing the good of the people both here and hereafter. Above all, he stressed the value of impartiality in justice and punishment. He also envisaged the state as an institution of universal benevolence and embarked upon an ambitious program of nation-building activities. He says that he had wells dug at every half a *Kos,* set up watering places for men and animals on the highways, had shade-giving Banyan trees and mango groves planted, put up raised seats for the weary travelers on the road, established hospitals for men and animals, and had medicinal herbs and plants brought and cultivated for the welfare and health of all beings. All this activity no doubt encouraged travel by traders and must have contributed to increased economic prosperity of his people. But the construction of public hospitals was a unique activity and marks Asoka as perhaps the world's first great philanthropic ruler. Asoka constantly thought of the welfare not only of men but also of animals and toward the end of his reign declared a number of quadrupeds, fish, and birds inviolable. To those people condemned to death he gave a grace of three days, though he could not bring himself to abolish the death penalty. For the slaves and the menials he recommended kindness and consideration at the hands of their masters, though he could not recommend the abolition of slavery altogether.[15] This is not strange, for though the

Buddha prohibited his order of monks and nuns from having anything to do with slavery, he was not in a position to bring about the elimination of a powerfully entrenched social and economic institution of his times. But it is to the Buddha's credit that in his writ, he had the courage to denounce human bondage.[16]

Asoka felt that it was his prime duty as king to supervise his administration at all times and prevent it from degenerating into an instrument of oppression and terror. He exhorted his officers to preserve their mental balance and dispassionately administer the rules and regulations laid down by him. They should particularly ensure that there would not be any unjustified punishments and imprisonments or unjust torture of citizens. To see that such abuses of power were prevented, he ordered periodic inspections of administrative arrangements in the provinces and the districts. He strove to make his administration as humane and benevolent as possible and dedicated himself to the welfare of his subjects at all times.

In all his administrative actions Asoka endeavored to enforce the dictates of morality, *dharma*. His concept of morality was a comprehensive one, as it touched upon not only the simple administrative actions and performance of works designed to increase the physical happiness of his subjects, but also aimed at the growth of a moral consciousness among them. He felt that it was his duty to look after not only the worldy interests of his citizens, but also their spiritual being, their social obligations, and filial behavior. He felt that the existing cadre of officers was inadequate to perform such comprehensive tasks and appointed a special class of officers called the *Dharmamahamatras,* or Morality Officers, in the thirteenth year of his reign (256 B.C.).

IV

Our main sources of information on the Asokan administration are his inscriptions and the book of Kautalya. Asoka's inscriptions, though very detailed in respect to information on his own philosophy, are rather sketchy about his administrative system. Kautalya's book is a theoretical work and, though its information is confirmed in many respects by the observations of Megasthenes, must be treated as such. Our picture of Mauryan administration under Asoka, therefore, is still not as complete as we would desire.

The three important branches of the administration were the military, revenue, and justice departments. Over all of them the king, in consultation with his council, exercised constant supervision. The Mauryan administration was noteworthy for its large army of bureaucrats in charge of the various departments of the administration. According to the Greek accounts the Mauryan military organization was entrusted to six boards, each with five members on it. First, there was the board for the infantry. The Mauryas were said to have maintained a large infantry force among their standing army of about six hundred thousand men during the regime of Chandragupta. The soldiers formed one of the seven important classes of Indian society, according to Megasthenes. This class numbered second only to that of the farmers and possessed "the greatest freedom and the most spirit. They practise military pursuits only. Their weapons others forge for them, and again others provide horses; others too serve in the camps, those who groom their horses and polish their weapons, guide the elephants, and keep in order and drive the chariots. They themselves, when there is need of war, go to war, but in time of peace they make merry; and they receive so much pay from the community that they can easily from their pay support others." Of the equipment of the infantry, we are informed by the Greek observer that "the infantry have a bow, of the height of the owner; this they poise on the ground, and set their left foot against it, and shoot thus; drawing the bowstring a very long way back; for their arrows are little short of three cubits, and nothing can stand against an arrow shot by an Indian archer, neither shield nor breastplate nor any strong armor. In their left hands they carry small shields of untanned hide, narrower than their bearers, but not much shorter. Some have javelins in place of bows. All carry a broad scimitar, its length not under three cubits; and this, when they have a hand-to-hand fight—and Indians do not readily fight so among themselves—they bring down with both hands in smiting, so that the stroke may be an effective one." [17]

The second board was in charge of cavalry. Very often this was the weakest part of the traditional Indian army. It was only by about the sixth century B.C. that cavalry became a recognized part of the army, and by the time Alexander the Great led his famous Macedonian horse into the Indian field, there were Indian cavalary units opposing his march. Perhaps for the first time in the military history of India the importance of cavalry was organizationally accepted by the Mauryas, who created a special board to look after the supply, training, and equipment of their cavalry. Kautalya has a whole section dealing with this subject in his *Arthashastra*. The sources for the supply of horses were the international and Indian markets, horses captured in war, and those locally bred. Among the best steeds mentioned by Kautalya are those that came from the northwestern areas of the country, like Kamboja.

The equipment of the horses, as mentioned by the Greeks, seems to be very inadequate. Bits and stirrups were not used, though there are some vague references to saddles. But these may mean blankets rather than true saddles. Post-Maurya sculpture, however, has representations of horses with full equipment, including reins, saddle, and stirrups. It may be inferred that such equipment came into general use after the Maurya age, though it is possible that it had already started with the Mauryas. There are also references to the bodies of the horses being protected by armor.[18]

The third board looked after the maintenance, equipment, and training of the war elephants, which were the most formidable-looking part of the army. Both the Nandas and the Mauryas, as well as the later rulers of India, possessed numerous war elephants, which made their strategy a static one of positions, rather than movements, in which they could be easily outmaneuvered by an enemy chiefly relying on the use of well-trained and well-equipped cavalry. This was the experience of Porus against Alexander, and this was also the plight of the Lodis who fought against Babur in 1526. Kautalya recommends the use of elephants largely for heavy work like construction of roads and destruction of enemy fortifications as well as for a show of magnificence. Each elephant carried three archers and a *mahout,* or driver.

The fourth board was responsible for the war chariots. There were as many as seven different kinds of chariots in use, and those specifically used in war are described as seven and one half feet in height and nine feet in width. Forty-five such chariots formed a unit and each was drawn by five horses. The chariot unit comprised 675 soldiers and an equal number of followers and servants. The work of the chariots, according to Kautalya, was "protection of the army; repelling the attack made by all the four constituents of the enemy's army; seizing and abandoning [positions] during the time of battle; gathering a dispersed army; breaking the compact array of the enemy's army; frightening it; magnificence; and fearful noise." [19] Each chariot carried one driver and two combatants.

To the traditional fourfold army the Mauryas added two new categories. These were the navy and the commissariat departments. India had a long naval tradition, and the skill and efficiency of Indian shipbuilders and sailors were amply demonstrated when Alexander impressed them into his service during his operations in the Punjab. Shipbuilding on a large scale was a government monopoly, and the Mauryas maintained naval units both for river-crossing and patrolling of the coastal areas. Kautalya recommends the appointment of superintendents for the various aspects of maritime navigation and for collection of tolls and dues. The Greeks mention a board of admiralty, which was in charge of the navy. This board, like the other departments of military organization of the Mauryas, had five members on it. The example of the Mauryas was followed by the Satavahanas and the Cholas and later by the Marathas. Indian ships ranged far and wide over the expanses of the Arabian Sea and the Bay of Bengal and carried extensive commerce to the countries of the Middle East and Southeast Asia. The spread of Indian culture to Malaya and Indonesia was largely due to the work of the Indian sailors, merchants, Kshatriya adventurers, Brahmin priests, and Buddhist missionaries using Indian ships. The commissariat board was responsible for supplies to the whole army. In Kautalya's account each branch is described as being under a superintendent.

Chandragupta, the grandfather of Asoka, is said to have maintained an army that numbered 600,000 infantry, 30,000 cavalry, about 8,000 (22,000 men) chariots, and 9,000 (36,000 men) elephants. The total number of men employed in the armed services was in the neighborhood of 690,000,[20] excluding the attendants and camp-followers, who would number at least another 20,000. This adds up to almost 1,000,000 men, which may be an inflated figure, but it would bear out Megasthenes' observation that next to the farmers the soldiers comprised the most numerous class in Indian society.

Besides the standing army Kautalya recommends the use of other types of armed contingents. Kautalya divides the armed strength of a king into six different types. These were the provincial army, the mercenaries, the guild-levies, the allied forces, troops recruited from the enemy's country, and the armed levies from the forest tribes. Asoka inherited a large army from his grandfather and father. As argued earlier in reference to the Kalinga war, Asoka continued to maintain this force at least until the eighth year of his reign. That he continued to maintain his vast army, even after he renounced force as a part of statecraft in external relations, seems obvious from the fact that nowhere does Asoka mention that he disbanded his army. There are certain obvious economic implications of the policy of maintaining large armies. First, large armies were necessary because of the continued existence of interstate warfare and the threat of such warfare in a country of continental dimensions. Second, the technological inferiority in the manufacture of equipment and weapons compelled the ruler to make up such deficiencies with large numbers. An army of one million men for a large empire like that of the Mauryas was perhaps nothing extraordinary. This army cost the exchequer in modern terms somewhere around £7,000,000, or about $20,000,000 a year.[21] This must have been a considerable burden for the population to bear, and the fact that it bore such a heavy burden is indicated by the numerous taxes and exactions devised by Kautalya. As stated earlier, in spite of the change in policy Asoka does not seem to have decreased his army, and the burden of supporting a large army must have been continued to be borne by the subjects of Asoka in spite of his pacifist intentions.

V

Estimates of the finances of the army should lead to a consideration of the financial administration of the Maurya Empire under Asoka. The backbone of public finance in Mauryan India, as in later times, was the agricultural revenue. Land was broadly divided into four categories. These were the crown lands, private lands, forests, and pastures. There has been a great deal of discussion on the nature of landownership in Mauryan India, and it has been stated by some scholars that all land belonged to the king. This could have been so only in a very qualified sense, though there is no doubt that the Mauryan administration controlled agricultural settlement and operations more or less thoroughly. Such a control also existed in other spheres of economic life, if we are to believe that the detailed regulations of Kautalya prevailed in the Asokan age. The Mauryas charged a twenty-five per cent tax on agricultural incomes. Asoka granted a special concession to the village of Lumbini, the birthplace of the Buddha, by reducing the impost to one-half of the usual. The rate charged to the crown lands must have been much more and may even have amounted to fifty per cent of the produce. The impost naturally varied according to the quality of the land and the availability of irrigational facilities, the expense of which was naturally charged to the beneficiary farmer. The rate charged was related to net income. Various charges were levied from those who collected the produce of the forests or grazed cattle. In fact, the number of imposts reflects the ingenuity of the Mauryan theorist, and this is of a very high order indeed! Besides the agricultural revenue, the state collected taxes from the working of mines and mineral products, industries, commerce, and, finally, tribute. An army of inspectors and supervisors was employed to ensure that there was no tax-evasion, and the taxes were collected punctually and in full. The average citizen of Mauryan India had his life well controlled by the state in a variety of ways. Industry and commerce, forests and pastures, lands and cattle, flowers and perfumes, travel and marketing, liquors and other intoxicants, almost every conceivable activity likely to produce income was taxed. Even the prostitutes and courtesans were made to yield a part of the proceeds of their calling.

Such collection of a multitude of taxes and rigid regulation of economic activity could only inhibit increased production. The expenses of a large empire were often ruinous, especially to trade and commerce, and Kautalya displays a particular antagonism to those engaged in large-scale trade and commerce. The Magadhan empires rode to glory over the backs of the commercial class, but the Mauryas seemed to have practically taxed this class out of existence. Kautalya recommends that the king arrange and control large-scale colonizing activities through the settlement of families of Shudras and others in virgin lands. This may be an indication of the fact that the limits of state expansion had been reached within the existing frontiers, and there were few prospects of increase in state revenues. This may have been due to the quality of the land or the industry of the people or to poor technological development. Increased colonization controlled by the state, therefore, was expected to increase the state revenues, which must have reached its taxable limits under the existing system in the settled rural and urban areas.

As in the other areas of administration the king was expected to be the fount of justice, charged with the responsibility of ensuring an efficient system of judicial administration. He appointed the highest judges and heard the final appeals. He exercised the rights of review and clemency and often spent a major part of his working day hearing representations from the subjects. There were two kinds of courts in operation, the civil court (*dharmasthiyam*) and the court of criminal jurisdiction (*kantakashodhanam*). There was an intricate and rather elaborate law of evidence, and ordeals were recognized as admissible evidence. In the provinces and the districts the provincial executive officers were also responsible for some aspects of the judicial administration, and it is in this respect that the possibility of bureaucratic oppression was the most frequent. There were cases of punishments involving fines and imprisonment in the provinces and the districts, and it was against such occurrences that Asoka exerted his personal influence on his officers through his royal edicts and tours of inspection.

The Maurya Empire was a paradise for the bureaucrat. Kautalya recommends the employment of scores of departmental heads, inspectors, and superintendents covering all aspects of public activity. In the Asokan inscriptions, the *Rajukas* seem to be the most important officers at the provincial and district levels. They are referred to in as many as five different inscriptions containing the emperor's exhortations to them. They are described as being in charge of many hundreds of thousands of people[22] and were granted discretion in the matter of bringing an accusation or plaint, or punishing offenders. The reason for such freedom of action, Asoka explains, is the necessity of creating a feeling of absence of fear and possession of confidence, so that the officers may exert themselves fully in making arrangements for the happiness and welfare of the people of the rural areas. They were to act as a link between the masses in the countryside and the king in the capital. The king insisted on impartiality in judicial pro-

cedure and in punishments. This is a remarkably early enuncia-
tion of the principle of "equality before law" and redounds to the
credit of Asoka, especially in view of the fact that the later law
codes like those of Manu negate it.

The Rajukas, therefore, appear to be highly placed executive
officers who also performed some judicial duties, especially in the
rural areas. They have been called "highest executive officers,"
"commissioners," "chief provincial revenue officers" and "district
officers." [23] The Rajuka, in view of his comprehensive and multifarious duties, was the kingpin of the administration in the rural
areas, and frequent contact between him and the emperor was
maintained by agents called the *Purushas*. The agents are described as of three classes, highest, middle, and low, and belonged
to the superior civil service. They were directly appointed by the
imperial headquarters and were responsible to them. They kept
an eye on the provincial and district officials, especially in the
matter of their loyalty to the king, and they maintained contact
with the common people to gage the public feeling in relation to
the several royal acts. They were thus intelligence officers who
also performed other supervisory duties.

Inferior in status to the agents were the *Yuktas*. They were ordered to go on a quinquennial inspection, and some of them were
also appointed in the department of accounts. They generally
functioned as district officers who kept accounts of revenue, and
"they also managed the king's property and had power to spend,
where expense was likely to lead to an increase of revenue." In
Asokan times they were also given the duty of spreading knowledge about the king's policy of righteousness and ensuring that
the royal will in this respect was implemented.

The other class of district or provincial officers was the *Pradeshika*. They were ordered to go on inspections every five years
and were accompanied in this by the Yuktas. The Pradeshikas
had both revenue collection duties and magisterial functions.
These officers corresponded roughly to the category of officials
known today in India as the Divisional Commissioner. Besides
their revenue and magisterial functions they also discharged
other responsibilities dealing with works of public utility like the
digging of wells. The Rajukas and the Yuktas worked as the subordinate officers of the divisional administrator, the Pradeshika.[24]
And then there were the high officers called the *Mahamatras*.

There were several categories of these officers, and their duties were as varied as was their size numerous. They functioned in an executive as well as supervisory capacity. Some of them were in charge of provincial administrations as those in Pataliputra, Kaushambi, Sarnath, Samchi, Suvarnagiri, Isila, Samapa, and Tosali. Others were in charge of supervising the conduct of women and were specially concerned with the promotion of the Asokan Law of Piety among them. There were also the Wardens of Marches (*Antamahamatras*), who were entrusted with supervision over the administration of the border areas and worked among the more backward sections of the population. They were also sent to the neighboring states to carry out Asoka's program of dharma.

In his Rock Edict V, Asoka speaks of the appointment of a special class of officers in the thirteenth year of his reign. The inscription states "In times past [officers] called *Mahamatras* of morality (*Dharma-mahamatra*) did not exist before. But *Mahamatras* of morality were appointed by me [when I had been] anointed thirteen years. These are occupied with all sects in establishing morality, in promoting morality, and for the welfare and happiness of those who are devoted to morality [even] among the Yonas, Kambojas, and Gandharas, among the Rathikas, among the Pitinikas, and whatever [other] western borders [of mine there are]. They are occupied with servants and masters, with Brahmins and Ibhyas, with the destitute, [and] with the aged, for the welfare and happiness of those who are devoted to morality, [and] in freeing [them] from desire [for worldly life]. They are occupied in supporting prisoners [with money], in causing [their] fetters to be taken off, [and] in setting [them] free, [if] one has children, or is bewitched, or aged, respectively. They are occupied everywhere, here and in all the outlying towns, in the harems of my brothers, of [my] sisters, and [of] whatever other relatives [of mine there are]. These *Mahamatras* of morality are occupied everywhere in my dominions with those who are devoted to morality, [in order] to ascertain whether one is eager for morality, or established in morality, or furnished with gifts." [25]

The inscription quoted above gives in admirable detail the scope of the activities to be pursued by these special officers. From their title it is clear that their institution was connected with the new policy of Asoka that he calls the Law of Piety. Now the term *dharma* has a variety of meanings, among which code of filial conduct, morality and religion are prominent. The Morality Officers of Asoka were concerned with each of these branches of dharma. They were to ensure that all sects lived in amity everywhere. This was particularly urgent in view of the reputed hostility between the Jains and Ajivikas on the one hand, and Jains and Ajivikas against the Buddhists on the other. Such hostility might easily lead to prolonged bitterness and disturbances of peace, and, in this context, the Morality Officers seem to have been responsible for the maintenance of peace and amity among the sects.[26] They were also to see that royal charity was evenly distributed and well-maintained. They were responsible perhaps for the maintenance of certain charitable public works, like the resting places for travelers on the highways. They were to see that undue hardships were not inflicted on the aged and the infirm, and that there was no miscarriage of administrative authority and justice. They were expected to supervise the actions of lesser officials. Among the adjoining territories on the borders of the empire they were supposed to carry out works of piety among a variety of tribes and peoples and to spread the Gospel of Piety as advocated by the emperor. Finally, they were expected to supervise morality in the families, not only of common people, but also the royal relatives in the capital city and the provincial towns. A formidable list of assignments indeed! For this they must have been armed with extraordinary powers of supervision, action, and punishment, and considering the long list of their duties their number must have been large. We have here, therefore, a picture of these royal officers being everywhere all the time, investigating not only public activities but also empowered to invade the privacy of households, royal and otherwise. The emperor was no doubt activated by the highest motives, but it is more than possible that his zeal created new opportunities of bureaucratic interference in the most intimate aspects of family life. We have no means of knowing how the people reacted to such enthusiasm on the part of their emperor, but it is likely that this innovation must have been silently resented by segments of the population in the urban areas. The Kautalyan state was already tightly regulating the economic life of the community; to that was added this innovation of regulation of religious, moral, and family life by Asoka in his quest to make the sway of morality universal.

The provincial government was either the responsibility of princes of the royal family (called by Asoka the *Aryaputras*)[27] or other high officers. These provincial governors had their own councils and provincial armies and were the emperor's eyes and ears in the far-flung parts of the dominions. The king's agents maintained a close contact between the emperor and his provincial administration, conveyed the imperial orders, and constantly checked on the loyal disposition not only of the princes but also of their subordinate officials. The Mauryas used a vast and intricate system of espionage to keep corruption down to the minimum and to prevent sedition everywhere. The royal spies swarmed everywhere and could be the third man when two were plotting.

The inscriptions also mention several other officials. One category was that of the *Vachabhumikas*, who were controllers of the cowpens. These officers controlled the pastoral settlements in the provinces and districts and collected the various cesses and imposts from them.[28] Then there is a mention of *Mukhyas*, who were chief officers of the various administrative departments. Finally, there was the *lipikara* (one Chapada is mentioned by name), the engraver of inscriptions, or the scribe who was responsible for putting into writing royal pronouncements.[29] Very often, the king gave oral orders that were later reduced to the required literary and official forms by the *lekhaka*, or writer, and engraved on stone or wood by the lipikara. The Mauryas maintained a large archival department storing diverse kinds of documents on revenue collection, judicial decisions, and royal decrees; and this required the employment of a large number of archivists, engravers, and writers.

The cities and towns in Mauryan India were important centers of administrative activity. By the fourth century B.C. India had witnessed a rapid growth of urban centers of population, and we know of at least sixteen cities and towns of Asokan India. These cities and towns contained places of vital economic activity like trade and commerce, manufacturing and industry. The Mauryan exchequer derived a sizable income from urban taxation, and urban administration had developed a high degree of complexity and sophistication. The officer in charge of urban administration was the *Nagaraka*, who was assisted by other officers called the *Sthanikas* and *Gopas*. These officers were responsible for the safety and security of the cities, regulation of trade and commerce, proper supervision of labor, industry, and taxation. They enforced the fire-safety and sanitary regulations, carefully watched the state of the roads and the highways, and were generally responsible for the welfare of the urban population. The cities were divided into wards, each of which was under the charge of a Sthanika. The wards were subdivided into units of households supervised by the Gopa.

Asoka mentions another class of officers concerned with aspects of urban administration, namely, the *nagalaviyohalakas*.[30] These had the rank of Mahamatras and were concerned with the administration of justice in the urban areas. They enforced the orders of the king in releasing prisoners on certain auspicious days. These Asokan officers may have worked under the general supervision of the Nagarakas but seem to have had special responsibility in the work of administration of justice and prisons. They may be described as the magistrates of Asokan times.

Megasthenes speaks of a very elaborate system of urban administration. He says that the city administration was in charge of six boards with five officers on each board. Each board had its own department and administrative staff. The first board supervised the work of industries, crafts, and trade-guilds. The second board was in charge of the inns, supervised the movement of foreigners, provided medical help for them when they were sick, and lawfully disposed of their effects when they died. This is an indication of a rather unusual influx of foreigners into the towns and cities of Mauryan India and is quite in keeping with the general picture of internationalism and cosmopolitanism of the Mauryan age. The third was a board of census that kept a careful census of births and deaths, obviously for the purpose of efficient administration and taxation. The fourth board was in control of the markets and was especially in charge of weights and measures. The fifth board inspected manufactured goods, attempted to prevent fraud and adulteration, and kept a careful eye on the movement of goods and their prices. The sixth board was concerned with the collection of taxes, which ranged from four per cent to twenty per cent.[31] Such an elaborate structure must have ensured an efficient administration and was indicative of the great economic activity in the urban areas.

VI

The picture of Mauryan administration as described above is one of a vast conglomeration of power manipulated by the dominant will of an emperor served by a large standing army and a fairly numerous bureaucracy. Such an administration could have arisen only in answer to certain specific needs of the times. We have referred earlier to the breakdown of tribal society and the emergence of regional societies in its place. These regional societies were still rather heterogeneous in their ethnic, economic, and social composition. To this heterogeneity was added the internationalism and cosmopolitanism of the Mauryas, which, if it made the diversity more interesting, also made it more complex and created new problems. With the breakdown of the traditional systems of social control the problem of administrative organization assumed new dimensions. New economic activity threw up new social classes, whose wealth was both beneficial and challenging to society and social order. There was also a decline in the moral norms guiding social conduct.[32] The growth of numerous sectarian theories created possibilities of religious feuds that could seriously disturb the peace of the realm. The tribal assemblies were effete, and the organs of autonomous urban control had yet to develop. This was an age of movement over areas and classes. In such an age of transition, when the traditional organs of control failed to exercise real power, it was natural that control would pass into the hands of the king and his bureaucrats. The king had not only to be the ruler but also the peacemaker, the prosecutor, and the judge. The new society needed not only a new centralized administration but also a uniform or homogeneous ethos. The Asokan attempt was to find solutions to the problem of achieving an equilibrium for the new and sometimes conflicting political and social forces, and it was in this that the Asokan administration assumed a new character.

The first two Mauryas had developed the essential structure of Mauryan administration, which closely resembled the theoretical injunctions of the *Arthashastra*. The observations of the Greeks reveal the organizational complexity and skill of this structure. Asoka inherited it and for the first ten years or so used it for the consolidation of his empire. After the Kalinga war there was a gradual change in his personal philosophy, and certain administrative changes were necessary to implement this changing view of the state and the purpose of life. The country, for him, now appeared to be a vast family over which he, the *pater familias,* presided. As the head of this extraordinarily complex and large family consisting of groups (*nikayas*) at various levels of civilization and social development, he had to devise a policy of toleration and unity. Indeed, Asoka seemed to be constantly preoccupied with the concept of unity, or *samavaya,* [33] as he called it. Politics for him was neither purely power (danda) and glory (*Aishvarya*) nor just an instrument of law and order; its purpose had to be something higher, which is called dharma. Now it is true that in the traditional scheme of ideals of life, as formulated and institutionalized in later works, dharma figures as the first of the four values, but it is one of four. For Asoka dharma meant everything, the highest value and perhaps the only value! This was a result of the Buddhist influence on his life, and it was this distinctively Buddhist legacy that he desired to enshrine through his own statecraft. He viewed life, all life, as one and indivisible and constantly revealed his preoccupation with the welfare of both men and animals. For the less privileged sections of society he felt a special concern and constantly exhorted his subjects to be kind and sympathetic to the servants and slaves. His thinking was all-inclusive, comprehending within its scope not only diversity of social classes, but also variations in the manifestations of life, human and animal. Discriminating intelligence (*pradnya*) and compassion for all beings (*karuna*) were the major foundations of his philosophy of life. He strove ceaselessly to realize these ideals in practice and hoped to live in the best Buddhist tradition of a counterpart of the Being of Infinite Compassion, the Bodhisattva, so well-known in Buddhist literature and philosophy. Finally, Asoka had set before himself the aim of making his administration so morally elevating for his subjects that the distinction between gods and men would more or less disappear, and the very gods would descend from their heavens to this world to rub shoulders with mere men. In his characteristic enthusiasm Asoka claimed that this great aim had now been realized.

CHAPTER VI

The Royal Philosopher

THE GREAT INTEREST OF THE ASOKAN STORY LIES IN THE EMPEROR'S fascinatingly rich personality. His reaction to war, his solicitude for the welfare of his subjects, his frank admission of not having done as much as he wanted to do both for himself and his people, lend to the account of his life a warm, human glow. In all of these Asoka stands unique. Equally unique is his world view, his Weltanschauung. He does not claim to be a philosopher but calls himself the "Beloved of the gods, of Gracious Mien," a sensitive human being who finds himself in possession of overwhelming power and attempts to extricate himself from his predicament by coming to moral terms with it. Buddhism made Asoka great; but it must also be understood that it was with Asoka that Buddhism turned away from its purely sectarian stance of being a more or less monastic sect into a force capable of transforming mere power into greatness. Asoka formulated his thoughts some twenty-two centuries ago; today they sound as fresh and relevant to the human situation as they were when they were engraved on primeval stones scattered about over the Indian subcontinent. His philosophy sheds a delightful light on his incredibly complex personality, and we shall now turn to an examination of this philosophy.

The "political philosophy" of Asoka must, however, be viewed in its historical perspective. The mentor of the Mauryan age was Kautalya, and Asoka, we must assume, was fully conversant with the philosophy of the *Arthashastra*. Kautalya was mainly concerned with power, its problems and security. The outward manifestation of power is force, and Kautalya completely believed that force is necessary in the conduct of human affairs. His view of human nature is rather dim, and for him, peace is but an interval between wars. His state exists for the fulfilment of worldly aims of acquisition, protection of what is acquired, enlargement of the existing acquisition, and distribution of the profits of acquisition. Finally, Kautalya does not mind if morality is sometimes sacrificed in the interests of the security of the state.

Asoka understood all this but seems to have felt that such a philosophy was not wholly adequate to meet the demands of his own situation. Asoka believed in the perfectibility of human nature and was concerned with devising means for the realization of worldly as well as otherworldly good for the human being. For Asoka, the state was not an end in itself but rather a means to an end higher than the state itself, namely, dharma, or morality. If Kautalya gloried in war, Asoka showed an abhorrence for it after the Kalinga conflict and renounced war as an instrument of state policy. Asoka was not against the protection of his existing acquisitions but insisted that new acquisitions be made through moral means (*dharma vijaya*). If for Kautalya the state was a punitive instrument, for Asoka it was an educative institution. For the dichotomy between force and morality, between Kautalya and Buddha, had existed for a long time. Asoka felt that his most glorious mission was to resolve this dichotomy and endow the mechanism of the Kautalyan state with a moral soul. The experiment was challenging and fraught with unpredictable results, but Asoka felt the risk was worth the effort.[1]

Superficially viewed there is little that is startling or new in the world view of Asoka. He speaks of principles that are as old as the first stirrings of human conscience recorded in religious literature the world over. He preaches virtues and values that are the stuff of which great religions are made. But Asoka's distinct contribution lies in the new integration that he sought to achieve between theory and practice, a new correlation between power and morality. For his speculations he takes the whole wide world as it exists, not as some theoretically perfect entity, and attempts to turn the microcosm of individual aspirations and effort into a universal experience. He frankly confesses that his speculations began with a terrible personal tragedy, a tragedy that was born of a victory on a battlefield. This victory could have been easily forgotten, even if it appeared as a tragedy to the victor himself, if it had been perceived only on the personal level of awareness. But Asoka universalizes his predicament, and it is this act of turning what was intensely personal into something that is recurrent and universal that his philosophy seeks its being. And there was another problem that confronted him, a problem associated with his status as an emperor. This great status, paradoxical as it may seem, imposed severe limitations upon him and introduced into his thoughts a running dialogue between imperial grandeur and spiritual glory. The practical problem before him was how to reconcile the needs of his new philosophy with the demands of his station in life. All life in the world, he seemed to realize, was at best a compromise, for life sets its own limits within which the ethical being, involved in the world of paradoxical choices, must act. But this compromise, he argued, must aim at being both moral and beneficial.

Asoka's first concern was the formulation of a philosophy pertinent to his own personal situation, that of a ruler. He wasted no thought on the why and wherefore of the state but took it for granted. He almost seemed to enjoy his personal control of that state. He was aware that he was no ordinary mortal, but a Caesar. However, Caesarism as a philosophy of life seemed inadequate to him. Power was exciting, but to be enduring power must be tempered by the infusion of ethical perception within the core of its being. Indeed, his philosophy is a remarkable instance of "the transformation of power by other values, cultural, social and moral." [2] How could he solve the dilemma of power? Power could exist only in its use and not merely as an abstract metaphysical principle. He knew that absolute power such as he possessed could corrupt absolutely, and that corruption of a sensitive individual's conscience, charged with the duty of exercising power, could be averted only through a public philosophy of universal moral responsibility. His personal creed, Buddhism, had made him conscious of the primacy of moral values, and it was now his task to work out a viable relationship between the demands of a Kautalya and the prompting of a Buddha. To this task he turned soon after his agonizing victory in the eighth year of his reign, in 262-261 B.C.

His first reaction to this frightful confrontation of the possibilities of power was both political and religious. Politically, war was inevitable so long as there existed a plurality of political wills. The dominant will must prevail over other and weaker wills. But if the exigencies of power must lead to inevitable conflict, there must be found another way to resolve the conflict of plural wills.

If politics divide, he seems to argue, then ethics must unite. To ethics, then, he turned in an increasing measure.

Asoka's insistence on the primacy of ethical values in reminiscent of some aspects of the Stoic philosophy. Antigonus Gonatas of Macedonia (276-239 B.C.), it should be remembered, was a contemporary of Asoka and a disciple of the philosopher Zeno (*circa* 320-250 B.C.). Zeno preached that ethics is all-important, and happiness may be secured by conforming to divine reason, which governs the universe. A comparison of the Stoic ideal of the state and the Asokan political philosophy reveals points of similarity and differences. In the sphere of morality Asoka, like the Stoics, believed that the highest good is goodness or virtue, that the moral path is the best way, and that man must be indifferent to pleasure or pain in practicing the highest ideal, which is that of duty comprehensively understood and assiduously followed. Now we know that diplomatic and cultural contacts between the Hellenic and the Indic worlds existed from the time of Chandragupta Maurya, Asoka's grandfather, and that some knowledge of Greek thought must have been prevalent in Mauryan India. On the other hand, some elements of Stoic ideas were present in India a considerable time before the Stoic philosophy began in the Hellenistic world. In his ideal of the world state, the Stoic believed "that there is no distinction between different members of the state," that "they are united by harmony with the Common Law immanent in the universe," and that "it is not compulsion but love which binds them together." These ideas have striking similarities with those of Asoka, though the Alexandrine concept of the world state "originated out of political expediency" and was born of the need for the inclusion of a medley of peoples and nationalities, whereas that of Asoka, "out of moral necessity." For Asoka it was supremely important to secure happiness among men, and the way to achieve that end was through inculcation of morality.[3]

Asoka was initially bewildered by the diversity that surrounded him. He comments reflectively on this many-sided world. If people are one as human beings, they are certainly different as townsmen and rural folk, as citizens and tribal people. All men, he may claim, are his children, but he was aware that they were not all alike. He had, therefore, to think on two levels. On the first level he could reflect on the world with all its common follies and foibles, sense and nonsense. He speaks of the propensity of the people to indulge in empty ritual and ceremonies, so immersed in everyday life and influenced by a variety of seemingly unseen and irrational forces. He says: "people perform various ceremonies on occasions of sickness, the weddings of sons, the weddings of daughters, the birth of children, and departure on journeys. On these and similar occasions people perform ceremonies." And then he adds with an indulgent chuckle: "But at such times the womenkind perform many, manifold, trivial and worthless ceremonies." He also speculates that "man is various in his wishes and various in his likings." But if in their solicitude for guarding themselves against the ill will of gods and godlings, sprites and demons, and in their basic fears, hopes, and urges men are the same everywhere, there are also significant variations based on status and clan, class and tribe. There are the rich and poor, servants and masters, slaves and slaveowners. The structure of human society and its balance can be preserved only if certain hierarchical relations are assumed and influenced by respect and compassion. He is conscious of his great empire which for him is the world, but he is also aware that in this great universe of power there live diverse groups of human beings, and that ultimately it is the human being that is of significance. He mentions tribes, clan-groups, and families as the basic units of social organization and strives to formulate rules of benevolent conduct for each. The state for him is the arch of this vast edifice of society, and it is in the station of the emperor that the diversity of multifarious groups must be fused into a unified ethical will. He asserts that all men are his children and seems to emphasize the word *all*. His concept of humanity, therefore, is universal in its scope, and the emperor, as the "universal" ruler, must be concerned with the complete and universal welfare of his subjects. This universality of the state, in its aspirations and actions, must be firmly based on something that is timeless, and that can only be law. His Buddhism had taught him that the ruler of rulers was dharma, that this law was not just the legitimization of the king's will, but the dictate of custom, usage, immutable justice (practiced as of old), and the eternal nature of power as righteousness.[4]

Asoka was not concerned *how* the state came into existence. Probably he was aware of both the Brahmanical and Buddhist theories on the origins of the state. The Brahmanical theories made either divine intervention or military necessity the factors leading to the birth of the state. Asoka did not seem to believe in any divine association for the state, though he called himself "Beloved of the gods." He mentioned the gods on occasion, though he did not claim any special dispensation received by him from them. In this he presents a refreshing contrast to the Brahmanical theorists and the rulers influenced by their speculations. The Buddhists had propounded a theory on the origin of the state explaining it as a "primitive" election based on an implied contract. It is probable that Asoka was familiar with this theory, though there is nothing in the evidence to indicate that he either accepted or rejected it.[5] As a practical philosopher, he was concerned with the state as it existed in his time and especially with the ideals of this state.

The supreme ideal of the state, according to Asoka, must be the realization of happiness both temporal and spiritual. He called this *kalyana* and claimed that he had progressed far in this direction.[6] This is difficult to achieve because of the natural propensities of men for violence, greed, ill will, passion, and hatred. The primary condition for the realization of universal and eternal happiness is unity of purpose and propriety of attitudes and actions (*samavaya* and *sampratipatti*).[7] Both unity and propriety are values in themselves. Unity could be based on tolerance and compassion: tolerance towards differing theological, metaphysical, and social systems; and compassion on the part of the privileged toward the non-privileged. This noble aim can be realized only through the instrumentality of dharma.

II

Asoka's inscriptions were called by him rescripts on morality, or *dharmalipi*. Perhaps there is no other technical term in the whole range of India thought with such diverse connotations as dharma. It has been interpreted as the fixed law of heaven and earth, as custom and time-honored conduct, as virtue and canon law, and a host of other things as well. In Buddhist parlance dharma, as an attribute of the state, means justice, law, and order, *Recht* as well as *Sitte*. In its political connotation dharma is related to economic welfare (*artha*), moral welfare (*dharma*), moderation (*matra*), time, age (*kala*), and society, social groups (*parishad*).[8] In the Brahmanical literature on the subject dharma is described broadly as a code of conduct, custom, usage, and law. It has been argued in Brahmanical thought that if property is the first acquisition of man through the state, dharma is the second, for dharma is sustained by the state through its sanctions. The term dharma is derived from the root *dhri,* which means to sustain, uphold, hold together. In its earliest form the concept appears as the Vedic cosmic order *(rita),* which was often equated with eternal truth *(satya).* Alongside of cosmic order the concept of dharma also evolves, and eventually comes to mean, custom, moral law, laws or duties in general, and what is right. Dharma, then, gradually develops as a code of right or moral conduct and is related, in ever constricted circles, to the world of humans, to the age, to the state, to castes and to stages of life. Asoka accepted the traditional meaning and the connotations of his times that were associated with the term dharma but only in parts. For him dharma meant "insights and precepts of religion and piety, it also means the principles and prescriptions of ethics and morality." [9] Dharma is eternal; it is good or a value, or perhaps the greatest value in itself. Its basis is in morality or character, *shila,* which is constituted of various elements. These are compassion, charity, restraint, firm faith, truth, purity, humility, forbearance, and non-violence. Since dharma is not possible for the non-virtuous, the primary duty for the king, his government, and for man in general is to cultivate the basic universal morality implied by the Pali term shila. We will now see how Asoka related this concept of morality to his own personal behavior as a king, and to that of his government and his subjects.

Soon after the Kalinga war Asoka declared that he would pursue conquest through morality rather than through the force of arms. This resulted in his renunciation of war as a policy of his administration. Kautalya mentions three kinds of conquests, namely, *"dharmavijaya* where the conquering king is satisfied with the mere acknowledgement of his suzerainty by the conquered, *lobhavijaya* where the aim of the conquering monarch is to covet the territory and treasure of the enemy and then continue him in his kingdom, and *asuravijaya* where the enemy is deprived of his kingdom, treasure, sons and wives, and is himself captured as a prisoner of war, or slain." [10] When Asoka turned to conquest through morality, he obviously renounced all desire for further territorial annexations and acquisition of the wealth, human and material, of the conquered; but he believed that he could still retain his supreme position through persuasion and moral superiority. This is also the traditional Buddhist view, in which the universal monarch is supposed to conquer the world, not by using force and weapons but through the power of his moral earnestness. Furthermore, the ideal Buddhist ruler does not exact tribute from the subordinate kings but simply advises them on the observance of the moral precepts. In this the inspiration for Asoka's concept of righteous conquest came from the Buddhist ideas rather than from the precepts of Kautalya. His missions to the border peoples and the Greek potentates were of the nature of this Buddhist concept of righteous conquest. Of their polite reception there can be little doubt, though it is quite another matter whether they were as effective as the emperor wished them to be.

Asoka began with the premise that it was completely proper for the state to act as an agency of moral transformation in the lives of citizens over whom it ruled. His argument seems to be that if the state is a human creation, and if human beings have a diversity of political, economic, cultural, and moral interests, the state must strive to help human beings fulfil their several aspirations. He was not interested in creating a religious state, but he had no hesitation in declaring the state he controlled as a commonwealth of morality. The primary instrument that such a state would naturally use would be law, since a moral state had to be, to start with, a state based on law that is eternal and universal. This law cannot distinguish, if it is to be true to itself, between one caste and another, between a Brahmin and a Shudra. In order to be moral and universal, this law must subscribe to the doctrine of equality in punishments and equity in procedure (*dandasamata* and *vyavaharasamata*); in other words, law to be moral must be uniform and universal and not just a code of tribes and classes suspicious of each other. He was also convinced that the law must not be a mere codification of royal wishes and whims but must be securely founded on a public consensus represented by immemorial custom, usage, righteous conduct of outstanding men, and reason. Asoka expresses this thought by using two key terms, namely, *dhammaniyamana* and *nijhati* (regulation by the Law of Piety, and consensus born of precedents and deliberative actions in the past). In the inscription where these terms occur, he states:

"in times past kings had this desire, that men might [be made to] progress by an adequate promotion of morality; [but] on the other hand, men were not made to progress by an adequate promotion of morality. How then might men [be made to] conform to [morality]? How might men [be made to] progress by an adequate promotion of morality? How could I elevate them by the promotion of morality? Concerning this king Devanampriya Priyadarshin speaks thus. The following occurred to me. I shall issue proclamations on morality, [and] shall order instruction in morality [to be given]. Hearing this, men will conform to [it], will be elevated, and will [be made to] progress considerably by the promotion of morality." [11]

This is a remarkable epigraph in many ways. With rare candor Asoka was conducting a dialogue that laid bare his deepest convictions and his plans for the development of morality in his realm. Asoka believed in "the principle of the ruler's moral obligation to ensure the complete and universal happiness of his subjects." In a sense, he tried to combine his Buddhist ethics with the Kautalyan administrative system he had inherited in order to establish what one author describes as an "educative state"; and the result was the emergence of a "Caesaropapism" in the history of Indian political ideas and institutions. In doing this he claimed to be no innovator, though it is likely that this was either humility on the king's part or his desire to claim that what others might regard as an innovation had the sanction of ancient custom behind it. This custom may have fallen into disuse because of non-implementation, and Asoka was only trying to retrieve it from complete oblivion. It is in this sense that he uses the term *shasana,* or law embodying prohibitory and mandatory regulations.[12]

III

The prohibitory orders involved a ban on several things. One was against sacrificial slaughter of animals. Two principles were involved in such an interdict. One was a spirit of skepticism about the validity of sacrifice as a form of effective prayer. The attack on sacrificial slaughter of animals enjoined by the *Vedas* was initiated by the Buddha. The Buddha declared: "If a man month after month for a hundred years should sacrifice with a thousand [sacrifices], and if he but for one moment pay homage to a man whose self is grounded in knowledge, better is that homage than what is sacrificed for a hundred years." [13] Following this belief in his personal life, Asoka ordered a drastic reduction in the use of meat in his royal kitchen, though he could not give up its use entirely. In the twenty-sixth year of his reign, 244-243 B.C., he published a long list of names of birds and animals that were not to be slaughtered on certain days of the year and month. Most of them, however, were not normally used for food, and this order may not have caused much inconvenience to the people. Asoka's second reason for prohibiting sacrificial slaughter was based on the general Buddhist view of the virtue of non-violence. Time and again the Buddha had declared that a good Buddhist must not destroy life and should practice the policy of non-violence toward all living beings. And to make this recommendation effective, the very first of the ten Buddhist commandments required that a Buddhist, layman or monk, should abstain from the taking of life. As time advanced, Asoka became very rigid in his ideas on non-violence and approached almost the Jainistic insistence on sanctity of all forms of life.

Another prohibitory order banned the holding of certain popular festivals. The reason for this ban was that Asoka saw many blemishes in such celebrations, though he was quick to add that he approved of certain other kinds of festivals. The festivals on which the king frowned obviously involved bacchanalian practices associated with spring celebrations and festivals in honor of certain popular divinities. At such festivals meat foods and spirituous drinks were served; and singing, dancing, and dramatic shows were performed to the delight of the masses. Such occurrences offended the moral susceptibilities of the pious ruler, though it stands to reason that the prohibitory order issued by him seriously infringed upon the right to merriment by the populace in its own way.

But Asoka was not only negative in his approach to the problem of public morality. His realm contained numerous religious sects, and there was the need for a spirit of tolerance and harmony among the votaries of the various sects. He set a personal example in this matter by honoring all sects impartially and allowing the religious leaders of these sects to reside wherever they liked in the empire. This was in sharp contradistinction with Kautalya's injunctions against free movement by ascetics and recluses. The reason adduced by Asoka for the freedom granted to all sects was that they preached and practiced purity and self-restraint, and hence all were working for spiritual uplift. The king denounced the practice of disparaging rival sects in order to glorify one's own persuasion. In this remarkable edict, aptly described as the "charter of toleration," Asoka says: "King Devanampriya Priyadarshin is honoring all sects; both ascetics and householders; both with gifts and honors of various kinds he is honoring them. But Devanampriya does not value either gifts or honors so [highly] as [this], [viz.] that a promotion of the essentials of all sects should take place. But a promotion of the essentials [is possible] in many ways. But its root is this, [viz.] guarding [one's] speech, [i.e.] that neither praising one's own sect nor blaming other sects should take place on improper occasions, or [that] it should be moderate in every case. But other sects ought to be duly honored in every case. If one is acting thus, he is both promoting his own sect and benefitting other sects. If one is acting otherwise than thus, he is both hurting his own sect and wronging other sects as well. For whoever praises his own sect or blames other sects,—all [this] out of devotion to his own sect, [i.e.] with the view of glorifying his own sect,—if he is acting thus, he rather injures his own sect very severely. Therefore concord alone is meritorious, [i.e.] that they should both hear and obey each other's morals. For this is the desire of Devanampriya, [viz.] that all sects should be full of learning, and should be pure in doctrine." [14] Such a sentiment would be remarkable for its spirit of universal tolerance in any age, but it becomes particularly noteworthy when we bear in mind the age in which it was issued, namely, the third century B.C.! When we remember the wars fought and the bloodshed caused in the name of religion in Asia and the West, our admiration for this great ruler cannot but be enhanced for his eclectic and tolerant spirit. Asoka never ceased to be an ardent Buddhist. But his devotion to his own faith did not blind him to the recognition of something significant in every sect. He did not stop merely with a declaration of the royal intent but, as noted elsewhere, created a special class of officers, one of whose duties was to enforce the toleration edict in all its implications. In his personal life Asoka admirably displayed conduct commensurate with his intention by bestowing charity on the votaries of all sects with strict impartiality. He insisted on respect for the Brahmins and the ascetics of the Jain and Ajivika faith as well as his own Buddhist Order.

Asoka believed that a state, in order to be called great, must strive for the material welfare of its subjects. We have noticed his concern for the comfort of travelers, his building of hospitals for men and animals, and his command that medicinal plants and herbs be planted for the relief of pain for all living beings. All these measures were designed to create conditions of prosperity and comfort for the people and must have contributed to the temporal well-being of his subjects.

IV

In the sphere of individual conduct Asoka prescribed a number of recommendatory and regulatory ordinances. The basis of this philosophy is admirably stated in his observation: "[to practice] morality is meritorious; but what does morality include? [It includes] few sins, many virtuous deeds, compassion, liberality, truthfulness, [and] purity." [15] This is obviously an echo of the teaching of the Buddha to the effect that "non-commission of all sin, acquisition of merit; purification of one's mind; this is the teaching of the Enlightened Ones." [16] But merit cannot be gained without endeavor (*utthana*), for life is a precious opportunity for creating happiness for oneself and others, here and now and in the next world. The king felt that he had not exerted enough in his duty to do everything possible for the welfare of all, though in a single lifetime he had accomplished more than most. He also exhorted his subjects to be ever mindful of their own faults before they took it upon themselves to discover the foibles of others, for there is nothing like constant self-examination for spiritual progress.

The king took it upon himself to guide his subjects in the path of dharma, the major elements of which were compassion, morality, humility, self-control, and charity. He also laid down a code of behavior for members of families and social groups, teachers and pupils, and friends and companions. The main object in life, Asoka said, is to eschew sins and evil tendencies in oneself like anger, passion, and pride. This requires a constant check on oneself, a perennial introspection and a positive attitude of charity. A good life is facilitated if one has few possessions and fewer wants. The king especially recommended frequent and respectful visits to learned elders of all faiths and a readiness to meet all their material wants by giving them gifts. During such visits one must consult with them on all matters of the higher morality and obtain from them guidance for the good life. It is noteworthy that Asoka stressed the importance of spiritual leadership in his quest for morality and did not set himself up as the supreme teacher of moral values.[17] We saw earlier that he did not approve of certain ceremonies, which he declared to be void of the morality. In the place of these ceremonies he recommended the ceremonial of dhamma (*dhammamangala*) in the following words: "But the following practice bears much fruit, viz. the practice of morality. Herein the following [are comprised], [viz.] proper courtesy to slaves and servants, reverence to elders, gentleness to animals, [and] liberality to Brahmanas and Sramanas; these and other such [virtues] are called the practice of morality." [18] Such a ceremonial is conducive to happiness not only here but also hereafter, for it begets endless merit. On familial relations Asoka attached great importance to respect for and obedience to father and mother, liberality to friends, acquaintances, and relatives, and respectful attention to teachers. In his view family relations must be based on regard, affection, and respect for the elders and love and concern for the younger on behalf of the elders. If such attitudes prevailed there would then grow the feeling of unity (*samavaya*), and it is only when the family is united by respect and affection that society can grow and prosper in morality.

In his philosophy of life Asoka laid great stress on the problems of the hereafter. As a pious Buddhist layman, he believed in heaven. He believed that the hereafter should concern not only the individual but also the government, which should encourage people to prepare themselves for the next world through good acts in this life. For this purpose he asked his officers to strive to inculcate in themselves and those in their care a sense of moral earnestness. He also ordered the display of certain edifying scenes, such as those depicting the heavenly abodes, the columns of fire, and elephants, and other divine spectacles.[19] Some of these are described in the Buddhist texts, and probably Asoka had his artists paint these scenes for public display to impress upon the popular mind the possibilities of the hereafter. He firmly believed in the law of *karma* and rebirth, and felt that it was the duty of everyone to be mindful of the opportunities of life and not to let the time pass without doing something for the good of himself and others. His code of morality bears such a close resemblance to that preached by the Buddha that it is obvious that he was constantly referring to the Buddhist code when he was preaching to his subjects. In one of his sermons the Buddha advises the householders to avoid four vices: destruction of life, taking what is not given, licentiousness, and untruth. The good householder must eschew the four motives of partiality, enmity, stupidity, and fear. He must further avoid taking recourse to the six channels of dissipation, namely, drinking of intoxicating drinks, frequenting the streets at unseemly hours, frequenting fairs, addiction to gambling, association with evil companions, and habits of idleness. He must not associate with four kinds of people: avaricious friends, men of words and not deeds, flatterers, and wasters. He should respect parents, teachers, and other elderly people, be kind to the younger and the inferior, and be charitable to friends and others who seek his help.[20] The Asokan dhamma, therefore, was basically the Buddhist creed as adapted by Asoka for his subjects, not all of whom were Buddhists. He attempted to prepare a common ground in morality for all of his subjects, including those who did not accept the Buddhist metaphysical and sectarian doctrines but could find no objection in the general Buddhist code of morality.

In his personal faith Asoka tried to live up to the tenets of his creed of Buddhism. He went on a pilgrimage of the holy places of Buddhism, to the place where the Buddha was born, the spot where he was enlightened, and the deer park where he preached the first sermon and "set in motion the Wheel of Law." At all these places he set up magnificent monuments that are great works of art, and to the village of Lumbini, the birthplace of the Enlightened One, he gave a special gift in the form of exemption from the payment of many of the customary taxes "because the Buddha was born here." In one of his inscriptions he expresses his reverence for the Buddhist Order and goes on to cite those specific discourses of the Buddha (now parts of the Pali canon) that he finds most rewarding and that he desires be constantly studied by the fraternity of monks and nuns as well as the congregations of laymen and laywomen. This epigraph is of interest in indicating the king's familiarity with the sacred texts of Buddhism, reading which he must have spent considerable time in his busy life. Buddhist tradition tells us that Asoka built a large number of monasteries and stupas, and, as discussed earlier, Pali tradition claims that the third Buddhist synod was held in the capital city of Pataliputra at the commencement of the eighteenth year of his reign (253-252 B.C.). Asoka's inscriptions indicate that the Buddhist Samgha was at this time threatened with schisms, and the king used his imperial office in threatening the schismatics with expulsion from the Order.[21] The Buddhist tradition asserts that the Order dispatched a number of missionaries to various parts of the empire and outside it, and among these missionaries were Mahendra and Samghamitra, the son and daughter of Asoka. These missionaries carried the gospel of the Buddha all over the subcontinent and beyond its borders, and it is permissible to assume that for this missionary work the Buddhist Samgha must have received aid from the great Asoka.

V

Let us now recapitulate the dominant ideas in Asoka's philosophy of life and action. He called this philosophy his *dharma*, which was certainly a species of ethical syncretism founded on the major premises of the Buddhist faith. Asoka declared that his main task was to illuminate, preserve, preach, and spread this philosophy among his subjects as well as people near and far. He wanted the lives of the citizens of his empire to be regulated in accordance with the principles of this philosophy. He endeavored for almost a quarter of a century to help the growth of this dharma and regarded the gift of it as the greatest gift of all. He made it the sheet anchor of his policy of the state and with its aid desired to conquer the world. This was his concept of the conquest of righteousness. The policy, it may be argued, was also beneficial to the empire, as it provided the central basis on which the diversity of creeds, classes, and regional societies could be built into a grand imperial unity, which, he fondly hoped, would last as long as the sun and the moon! Religious toleration, social harmony, respect and affection in filial and group relations, nonviolence, and a respect for all living beings were some of the major aspects of this policy. Above all, the Law of Piety appeared to him as the only adequate substitute for a regimen of force, the only way to tame power and to transform it from an instrument of despotism into an agency of morality and welfare for his people. Was he inspired in this purely by wholesome ethical motives, or were there some political ambitions which it was made to serve? It has been remarked that Asoka made use of his dharma in consolidating his empire; that he used Buddhism, the core of his dharma, as a political instrument in making his subjects docile and subservient to the imperial will. For, it has been stated, "the ascetic preachers had now become far cheaper agents of law and order than the all-powerful stipendary officials backed by well-paid soldiers and checked by still better-paid spies." [22] It is possible that the policy of dharma was also politically beneficial, but on the available evidence it is too much to argue that Asoka conceived of it purely as a political instrument and used it as a well thought-out "Kautalyan" design for the subjugation of his people. If he desired glory, it was all too human; but Asoka makes it plain that the kind of glory that he wished for himself was far different from the schemes and plans of the common run of despots and dictators. The king's desire was to serve the universal humanity by proposing ethical solutions to problems of social and religious relations. He was working out a great experiment of founding a righteous state that could be an agency of welfare here and now as well as in the hereafter. Above all, he was in search for a solution to the problem of absolute power that, if left unchecked, he knew would not only destroy himself but his realm as well. Kautalya, in recommending the use of the police, armies, and spies, had indicated that eternal suspicion was the price of power. Asoka had tried that out up to the war of Kalinga and had found it deficient as a policy for a great state. Asoka's formulation of his own philosophy of dharma was a rejection of the earlier Kautalyan policy of the systematic use of fear and force, of making use of religious beliefs for increasing the power of the ruler, and of making the ruler live a life in which he was afraid of his own shadow. For Kautalya, state relations were primarily relations of power; for Asoka, they were pre-eminently human and ethical relations. This is the significant difference between the Kautalyan and the Asokan states, and this difference stems from distinct philosophical premises in each case. Asoka's kingdom of righteousness may not have lasted long after his demise, but the experiment in opening new dimensions in political philosophy was well worth it. In launching such a bold experiment Asoka was far ahead of his times, but if his experiment in righteousness was a political failure, it was also a grand moral venture. As we read his rescripts, the voice of Asoka comes trailing across the centuries, the voice of a king who had turned philosopher and a promising conqueror who had become an ethical preacher, telling us that if humanity can create vast power, it can also think boldly and transform that power into an instrument for raising itself, albeit temporarily, to newer heights.

CHAPTER VII

Culture of the Asokan Age

THE AGE OF ASOKA IS ONE OF THE GREAT PERIODS OF INDIAN HIS-
tory. The Maurya Empire was not only one of the largest India
has ever known but also perhaps the most efficiently adminis-
tered. And, above all, there is the personality of Asoka, unrivaled
in its human interest, lofty in its aspirations, and significant in its
achievements. We have already dealt with the various aspects of
his personality and will now turn our attention to the social con-
figuration, economic organization, and cultural attainments of
his empire.

The first fact that strikes us is the degree of urbanization
achieved by the country during the Mauryan age. At the very
outset we had occasion to note the commercial revolution that
preceded the birth of the Magadhan empires. This commerical
revolution created new urban centers of trade and industry based
on a surplus of manufactured goods and commodities to be exchanged virtually all over the country. The rapid spread of the
use of currency facilitated this revolution and created a new class
based on new forms of wealth. This trend toward increased urbanization continued throughout the Maurya age, and we know
of sixteen large towns and cities from Asoka's inscriptions. Most
of them were built on high ground in the plains or along river
banks and controlled the vital trade routes in the area. Kautalya
speaks of the organization of the cities into wards and units of
households, and we have already referred to the rather elaborate
civic administration devised by him for the cities. These cities
were bustling with trade and industry and contained the homes
of the more prominent of the king's subjects. The houses were
mostly built of wood and bricks and contained numerous items of
furniture necessary to comfortable living.

Of these cities Pataliputra was naturally the foremost. It was
the imperial capital and had palatial buildings, broad streets,

gardens and parks, and places of amusement. It was the nerve center of the empire, and from here were carried the orders that affected the lives of the people in the far corners of the country. Besides Pataliputra, there were many other fine cities. One of these was Taxila located in the far northwest. It is described as "large and has most excellent laws; and the country that lies round it is spacious and very fertile, immediately bordering also on the plains." [1] It was a center of trade and commerce, and by it passed important trade routes linking India with Central Asia on the one hand, and Persia on the other. It was often visited by ascetics and Buddhist monks, and the Greek observers were struck with the sight of these ascetics practicing austerities in the hot Indian sun. They also noticed the customs of polygamy and *sati* (self-immolation of widows) and the Iranian practice of the disposal of the dead by exposure to the vultures. After its conquest by the Mauryas it became an important viceroyalty, and Asoka, as we have noticed earlier, was sent there to quell a rebellion. The excavations at Taxila have revealed the extensive area occupied by the city and the imposing Buddhist monuments, such as the Dharmarajika stupa, dating back to Asokan times.[2] Turning southward, there was the city of Shakala (Sialkot in the Punjab), and the Buddhist work *Milinda Panha* grows lyrical over its description. Though it is possible that Shakala assumed its prosperous character after the downfall of the Mauryas, it is reasonable to hold that it already existed in Asokan times as a town of some importance.

On the western coast there were the cities of Bharukaccha and Shurparaka. Bharukaccha, Barygaza of Ptolemy (in the vicinity of modern Broach), was a well-known port from which ships sailed to Southeast Asia as well as to the Persian Gulf area. It was served by the rich hinterland of Gujarat and Saurashtra, and it is possible that scattered Buddhist communities had already existed there before the time of Asoka. The administrative headquarters of the Saurashtra region was at Girinagara (modern Junagadh), where Asoka had a set of his edicts inscribed on a rock. Girinagara was served by a large reservoir, and we know the names of Pushyagupta and Tushaspa, Mauryan governors, ruling there during the time of Chandragupta and Asoka.

Further down along the coast was Shurparaka, the seaport town thirty-seven miles north of Bombay, where a fragment of

Asokan inscriptions was discovered. It was probably the seat of the provincial government. It was connected with the Maharashtra region by trade routes that passed through the Western Ghats, probably along the routes indicated by the group of Buddhist cave temples at Kanheri (on the outskirts of metropolitan Bombay), Karle, Bedsa and Naneghat excavated after the time of Asoka.

In central India lay the city of Ujjayini, where Asoka served for a long time as a viceroy. Not far away was the town of Vidisha where he met Devi, who became his first wife and the mother of Mahendra and Samghamitra, the well-known Buddhist missionaries to Ceylon. Vidisha was an important Buddhist center and is the site of the famous Buddhist stupa that enshrined the relics of some of the most famous of the Buddha's disciples. Vidisha must also have been a town of considerable commercial importance, connected as it was with trade routes running east and west as well as south. In the east and south were the towns of Toshali and Samapa, Suvarnagiri and Rishila, where Asokan inscriptions have been found.

Gangetic India had a number of rich cities. Kaushambi and Shravasti were already old cities when Asoka arrived on the historical scene. These cities figure prominently in the social and economic history of India at the time of the Buddha, and, in addition to their commercial importance, they also prided themselves on the sanctity associated with the presence of the Buddha. Gaya, where the Buddha was enlightened, Sarnath (near Banaras), where he preached the first sermon, and Kapilavastu, near where the Master was born, were great centers of pilgrimage for the Buddhists; and Asoka visited all of them and left the mementos of his visit behind in the form of pillars and inscriptions.

The find-spots of Asokan inscriptions also indicate a few other important towns. Viratanagar (Bairat in Rajasthan) and Abhisara (Mansehra, in the Hazara district of West Pakistan) are two of them. But obviously there must have been many more of which we do not know.

Of the life of the people in the towns and cities the classical accounts give us some information. People, we are told, wore cotton and silk garments. One covered the lower part of the body while another was thrown across the shoulders. A third strip was wound round the head as a turban. Many wore gold and ivory rings, and quite a few decorated themselves with beards dyed in various colors. They carried sunshades and wore gaily colored and rather high-soled sandals. They were thin and tall and "much lighter in movement than the rest of mankind. They usually ride on camels, horses and asses; the richer men on elephants. For the elephant in India is a royal mount; the next in dignity is a four-horse chariot, and camels come third; to ride on a single horse is low." [3] The reference to people riding asses is interesting, for in later ages such a ride was considered a disgraceful punishment when ordered to be performed ceremonially!

A brisk and extensive trade was carried on in these towns and cities. Kautalya's *Arthashastra* reveals the extent and variety of this trade. There were regular built-up market places thronged by merchants from near and far bringing goods and commodities from the countryside as well as regions outside India. The most important articles of trade were cotton textiles, silk, woolens, hemp, metal utensils, agricultural implements, perfumes, liquors, hides, and skins. [4] The Mauryan state derived considerable revenue from taxation on trade, commerce, and industry; and the picture that is presented in the literature of the times is one of prosperity.

Amusement and relaxation formed an important part of urban life. The fairgrounds were crowded on special days, and there dramatic shows, acrobatic spectacles, singing, dancing, and puppet shows were held. Itinerant singers and dancers thrilled the audiences with their art, and the shops selling liquors and dainty and toothsome foods did a thriving business on these days. The samajas, or outings and picnics, were very common, and even royalty was supposed to patronize them to show its support of popular festivals. Asoka, after his conversion to Buddhism, decided to discourage the bacchanalian practices prevalent at these samajas and substituted in their place spectacles of religous import showing scenes from heaven and hell. How relaxing these were found by the crowds we have no means of knowing!

II

Outside the cities sprawled the countryside, the *Janapada,* clustered with towns and villages. Asoka paid particular attention to the welfare of the Janapada and spent considerable time paying visits to "the people of the country." The provincial towns were governed by semiautonomous assemblies whose work was supervised by royal officers. On villages and village life Kautalya presents some very interesting ideas. He recommends the formation of new villages with five hundred Shudra families protected by forts and boundary guards. Access to these villages was prohibited for ascetics, strangers, outside guilds, dancers, singers, drummers, clowns, and bards who were not natives of the village. This, indeed, is regimentation of village life. Asoka seems to have relaxed some of these restrictions, for he allowed ascetics to dwell everywhere.

Agriculture was the main occupation in the villages. Arrian states that the tillers of the soil formed the most numerous class of the population of the country. He further states, "they are neither furnished with arms, nor have any military duties to perform, but they cultivate the soil and pay tribute to the kings and the independent cities. In times of civil war the soldiers are not allowed to molest the husbandmen or ravage their lands; hence, while the former are fighting and killing each other as they can, the latter may be seen close at hand tranquilly pursuing their work, perhaps ploughing, or gathering in their crops, pruning the trees, or reaping the harvest."

This may sound as a lyrical description of rustic peace and contentment. But the other side of the picture is rather grim. The farmers, who formed the majority of the population, were disarmed, and their lives were regimented. They were bound to the land and their profession, for it was forbidden by custom to change occupations. As Arrian puts it, "One cannot, for instance, become a husbandman if he is a herdsman, or become a herdsman if he is an artizan." [5] And custom also prohibited intermarriages between the groups.

Here, then, we have a picture of the emerging caste system. The history of the caste system is complex and long, but it may be reasonably assumed that it came into existence, more or less in the form in which we know it today, sometime during 200 B.C.-200 A.D. Asoka's inscriptions mention a few such groups. These are Brahmin who are classed along with the *Shramanas* (homeless wandering ascetics). For these Asoka has nothing but respect, and he urges his subjects to treat them with generosity, respect, and consideration. But there were also other kinds of Brahmin who were householders, and who practiced a variety of occupations

such as priestcraft, agriculture, and civil service. The Greek observers mention seven castes among the people of India. Though
there is evidently some confusion in their understanding of the
situation, the picture presented by them is interesting as reflect-
ing the social reality of the Mauryan age. Of these castes the first
is the "Sophists who are not so numerous as others, but hold the
supreme place of dignity and honor,—for they are under no necessity of doing any bodily labor at all, or of contributing from
the produce of their labor anything to the common stock, nor
indeed is any duty absolutely binding on them except to perform
the sacrifices offered to gods on behalf of the state. If any one,
again, has a private sacrifice to offer, one of these sophists shows
him the proper mode, as if he could not otherwise make an accept-
able offering to the gods. To this class the knowledge of divina-
tion among Indians is exclusively restricted and none but a soph-
ist is allowed to practice that art." Furthermore, these "sages go
naked, living during winter in the open air to enjoy the sunshine,
and during summer, when the heat is too powerful, in meadows
and low grounds under large trees, . . . They live upon the
fruits which each season produces, and on the bark of trees,—the
bark being no less nutritious than the fruit of the date-palm." [6]
There seems to be some mixing up of details pertaining to the
Brahmanical priests and the Shramanas and Brahmins of the
Asokan inscriptions. If we are to believe the Pali texts, the Brahmins had also emerged as a distinct class, some of whom owned
large tracts of land to farm, for which they had to use paid and
bonded labor.

The classical observers next mention the warrior caste, which
was second in point of numbers to the husbandmen. These warriors perform only military duties, are paid well, and live in
comfort. The "warriors" may be the Kshatriyas, second in the traditional list of castes in India. It is not clear whether these Kshatriyas had already developed into a rigid caste. Besides the Kshatriyas, there were other classes, one of which was that of the
Ibhyas, an aristocratic class that ranked after the Brahmins and
Kshatriyas. These may be the wealthier section of the mercantile
and banking community. Then came the Shudras, whose occupations were closely and rigidly prescribed. They had become the
farming class, and some of them may have performed occupations
of artisans. As we saw previously, they were unarmed and bound

to the soil and occupation. They therefore represented a semi-servile class conveniently exploited by the state and its minions. They could be forcibly settled in villages, and their life rigidly governed by immemorial custom and state regulations.

Asoka often mentions two classes of people and recommends proper treatment for them. These were the *dasas* and *bhatakas,* slaves and hirelings. Slavery had existed in ancient India since pre-historic times. It was an established institution in the Indus civilization. The *Rig Veda* is replete with references to slaves taken in war against the non-Aryans. But even Aryans could be taken into slavery for various reasons. The Pali *Jatakas* describe slavery as a quite common institution. Slaves are of several kinds: some are born into slavery, others seek protection through it, many become slaves voluntarily, and quite a few could be bought in the market. They were also taken in war, and there are cases of even Brahmins and royal ministers being sold into slavery. Slavery was so common that even people of modest means could afford a slave. Kautalya has a long section dealing with slavery. He mentions nine different classes of slaves and lays down detailed rules for their treatment and manumission.[7] Generally speaking, the treatment of slaves was very humane, and the institution probably did not play a crucial role in the economy of the country, at least in historical times.

On the periphery of the sedentary society lived the forest tribes. First, there were the herdsmen, and "these neither lived in cities nor in villages but they are nomadic and live on the hills. They too are subject to tribute, and this they pay in cattle. They scour the country in pursuit of fowl and wild beast."[8] These fishermen, hunters, and trappers occupied the lowest rungs of the social and economic ladder along with those who collected the forest produce and worked in bamboo and cane. Ceremonially they were regarded as "untouchables." Asoka mentions the *atavijanas* for whom the emperor showed special solicitude, and these approximate to the class referred to above.

Asoka's policy of conciliation towards the forest tribes indicates a vital process going on within Indian society through the ages. These tribes, called "guest peoples" by Weber, lived on the periphery of the advanced population, for whom they were a valuable, numerous, and willing source of labor. The economic life of the forest people was threatened by the encroachment of the ad-

vanced economic system of the ever increasing settled areas, and
the problems of economic security and social status confronting
them was solved by their gradual fusion into the general Indian
society through their assimilation into the emergent caste structure. For this the tribal groups had to submit to the external con-
trols of the caste system, but in return there were the compensa-
tions of a relatively well-defined role in the new economy and a
well-determined place in the new caste society. This process went
on in a variety of ways, among which was the conquest of tribal
areas, and it was this instrument of war that was brought into
prominence during the Kalinga conflict waged by Asoka.[9]

Another characteristic of the society of the Asokan age we
might mention here was the prevalence of a large number of
tribes governed by their own customs and laws and enjoying a
degree of autonomy that could have been the envy of the imperial subjects. Many of these, like the Cholas, Cheras, Pandyas,
and Keralas, as well as the Gandharas and Kambojas, lived outside the limits of the imperial administration and hence were independent peoples. Others, like the Andhras, Pulindas, Bhojas,
Rashtrikas, and Petinikas, lived within the limits of the empire
(Rock Edicts II, XIII). They, however, must have been left
largely to the devices of their own organization, while the imperial administration contented itself with ensuring that there was
no overt disloyalty among them, and that the tribute was paid
regularly. And these tribal peoples must have realized, after wit-
nessing the plight of the Kalingas, that it was better to submit to
the great empire and suffer a partial diminution of their independence than to oppose it and have their lands devastated by
the imperial armies. The existence of these numerous tribal
groups shows a phase of transition from tribal to national society,
to complete which Asoka devoted strenuous efforts in his reign of
some forty years. That he did not completely succeed in his task is
proved by the re-emergence of the tribes after his death, followed
by the rapid disintegration of his empire.

III

From the foregoing it is clear that the social situation during
the Mauryan age, though rather fluid in its mobility, was approaching the status of a caste society. The two important characteristics
of the caste system, namely, fixed occupations and endogamy,

were already present. Ideas of ceremonial purity and impurity were slowly becoming indices of social status, and the beginnings of "ritual impurity," which later led to the development of the institution of untouchability, could already be seen. There was also a growing vegetarianism, for Arrian states that the people of India "live upon grain and are tillers of the soil; but we must except the hillmen, who eat the flesh of beasts and chase." [10] Asoka speaks of the numerous animals slaughtered for curry in the royal kitchen and says that he had almost given up the use of meat in his diet after his conversion. This general trend towards vegetarianism may have been due to the influence of the philosophies of non-violence as preached by Buddhism and more especially, Jainism. On the other hand, the influence of economic factors cannot be ruled out entirely. A large-scale use of meat requires large areas for grazing and pasturage. We have evidence of large tracts of forests where wild animals abounded, but as mentioned earlier, the class of herdsmen was numerically very small. There is some evidence of overcrowding in the country, though this must be taken only as relative and not absolute in terms of population figures. The available areas certainly seemed to be populous, offering much cheap labor. With such relative overpopulation, large-scale cattle rearing and dairy farming could be difficult and result in a general high cost of meat and dairy products. Furthermore, since agriculture was highly productive, agricultural products must have been relatively cheap. With these economic factors added to the influence of the concepts of non-violence and ceremonial purity and impurity developed by Jainism and Buddhism and the emergent Brahmanism, we can easily understand the general trend towards vegetarianism.

Life, it seems, was becoming rather austere. The tendency towards vegetarianism was paralleled by another that frowned upon the use of liquor and intoxicating drinks. As the fifth commandment shows, the Buddhists had forbidden the use of liquors and wines to their followers. The Jains also prohibited the use of liquor. Among the Brahmins there was an increasing tendency to discourage liquor, and soon after the Mauryan age it was considered ceremonial pollution for a Brahmin if he drank liquor. A Brahmin woman, according to Patanjali (*circa* 150 B.C.), who drank liquor was deprived of her husband's company in the next life.[11] According to Megasthenes spirituous drinks were served only at religious ceremonies; this is not borne out by Kautalya's observations. However, if we are to believe the *Arthashastra*, drinking was still a fairly common custom, and the state derived a considerable revenue from it. Liquor was sold not only in forts but also in "country parts." Liquor could be sold to persons of "well-known" character in stated quantities which could be taken out of the shop. Liquor shops were to be kept neat and clean and made attractive with perfume, flowers, and other comfortable things. This state of affairs may have rapidly changed during the time of Asoka. The trend of abstention from liquor grew rapidly after Asoka's time, and by the beginning of the Christian Era liquor seems to have been inadmissible, at least for the Brahmin caste. The Kshatriyas and others were free to drink, however.

The farmers grew two or three crops a year. Of these the winter crops were rice and millet; wheat and barley were grown in summer. Kautalya mentions a third crop of *Mudga* and *Masa* (pulses and lentils) grown in between the two main crops. Six varieties of rice were cultivated, and barley was grown or collected in a wild state. Barley was used for making gruel and cakes. Wheat and rice were the staple food in most of the areas of the country. As previously noted, this cereal food was supplemented with meat and fish. The dairy products in use included milk, butter, curds, and buttermilk; strangely enough, buttermilk was recommended for dogs and pigs. Food was also highly seasoned with pepper, mustard, coriander, cloves, turmeric, cardamom, spikenard, cinnamon, and vinegar. Sesame oil was used for frying. The cooking and eating utensils and plates were made of copper and bronze, and the rich supped off golden plates placed on low stools. Already the distinction between the rich and poor in the matter of diet is apparent, for the Greeks rather naively remark that the good health enjoyed by the common Indians was largely due to simple food and abstinence in the use of wines and other beverages.[12]

Such, then, is the general picture of social and economic conditions during the age of the great Mauryas. The level of the material civilization was undoubtedly high, and the general economic condition of the people was such that food, clothing, and shelter, the bare necessities of life, were sufficient for a fairly comfortable life. Theft was remarkably rare, and the general impression gathered by the Hellenistic observers was one of probity and honesty on the part of the people. As remarked earlier, there was a degree of social mobility horizontally as well as vertically, though the rules of castes were now becoming more and more intrenched. The largest number of restrictions naturally applied to the Brahmin caste. A Brahmin could not sell sesame oil, fish, or meat and was expected to abstain from the use of alcoholic beverages.[13] There was, thus, a growing spirit of austerity and puritanism. The preoccupation with ideas of ritual purity and impurity and the austere spirit of Buddhism and Jainism were the major factors in the development of sumptuary and dietary laws. It is permissible to argue that whereas the level of ethical awareness, if not of achievements, grew under the imperial prodding of Asoka, ordinary life appeared rather drab and monotonous to the man in the street, who may have wondered where the emperor was going and where it was all going to lead! Life was certainly highly regimented, not only by the numerous rules of Kautalya but also under the influence of the father image projected by Asoka. Since in his way of thinking all men were his children, it was his duty to tell the children what to do and what not to attempt. But perhaps we are trying to project our modern ideas into a past that accepted without question or demur such regulations and appreciated the intentions of the emperor, which were unquestionably of the highest order.

IV

The economy of the Maurya Empire was based on flourishing industries and extensive trade and commerce. It had long passed the stage of barter, and currency was now the medium of exchange. We have already referred to the wide prevalence of coins as a unit of exchange in economic transactions during the time of the Buddha himself. The *Jatakas* (the core of which has been ascribed to pre-Buddhistic times) frequently mention several kinds of coins. At the top, in terms of value was the *nikkha* of gold (the term itself goes back to Vedic times). Next to it was the *suvanna,* followed by the *masaka* and the *kahapana,* the last being made of silver or copper. Then there were the other coins described as the *addha,* the *pada,* the *addhamasaka,* and the *kakanika.*[14] Everything was now valued in terms of money, indicating that the stage of money economy had already been established by the fifth century B.C. This does not mean that the system of barter has disappeared completely, for it may well have prevailed in the remote or backward areas.

Who issued these coins? It was once argued that most of them were issued by individual bankers or trade guilds. This may well have been so in the beginning. But by the time the Nandas came on the scene, currency seems to have been taken over as a royal prerogative, which may have been delegated to certain regional or individual authorities by the central power. Kautalya in his *Arthashastra* refers to two officers connected with the issuance and circulation of currency. These were the Mint-Master and the Examiner of Coins, (*Laksanadshyksha* and *Rupadarshaka*). It was the duty of the Mint-Master to supervise the manufacture of silver coins made of stated parts of copper, silver, and alloys. From the detailed description given by Kautalya it is clear that coinage was a royal monopoly, and that currency was strictly regulated according to centrally adopted standards of manufacture.[15]

Patanjali, a grammarian of the second century B.C., also gives us information about currency. He mentions the *nishka, shatamana, suvarna, sana,* and *karshapana* with its subdivisions as units of monetary value.[16] He also refers to moneylenders, rates of interest, and payment of debts. Thus, from about the fifth century B.C. to the second century B.C., we have detailed evidence of the existence of currency, its values and circulation. The introduction of currency, the methods of its manufacture, and the marks on it began in India independently, though there was evidently a Persian and Hellenistic influence on certain aspects of Indian numismatic history. The early coins were manufactured in two forms, namely, punch-marked and cast. Punch-marked coins have been found from numerous sites in many parts of India, and the marks on them have been studied in detail by many scholars.[17] Attempts have been made to identify certain signs with rulers of the Nanda and Maurya dynasties, and in some cases the arguments appear rather conclusive. Thus the suggestions that the symbol of the peacock on the hill may stand for the Mauryas, and that another called the crescent on the hill and a third called tree-in-railing stand for Chandragupta and Asoka, respectively, appear plausible. Archaeological evidence from the Bhir Mound at Taxila and Uttar Pradesh confirms some of these suggestions since the period during which these coins were in circulation coincides with the period of the Mauryas. The find-spots, symbols, and variety of the coins unearthed from sites in northern and eastern India support the conclusion that these coins were issued under a central authority of the empire. The centralized empire facilitated the circulation of the currency on a national scale, which in turn helped trade and commerce to move from one area to another with great ease.

This ease of movement was further helped by the existence of long and well-recognized trade routes connecting different parts of the country. We have already referred to some of these trade routes and to the grand trunk road connecting Taxila with Pataliputra. Asoka undertook a vigorous policy of planting shade-giving trees along these highways and also set up rest houses and wells for drinking water for travelers and their beasts of burden. These were undoubtedly philanthropic acts, but they also facilitated travel for trade and must have brought increased revenue to the imperial exchequer. Traders now not only traversed the national highways but also exchanged their commodities at the terminal points for international trade such as Taxila. Asoka's policy of maintaining a "universal" empire, of providing it with easy and comfortable roads and trade routes, of vigorous police and judicial administration, and his own personal interest in even the most distant areas, must have broken down the provincial barriers and helped create a national culture influenced by the ideals of the emperor.

V

In the field of religious literature the Asokan age saw some significant developments. In his Bairat Stone Inscription Asoka refers to a number of texts from the Buddhist Scriptures and recommends them to the monastic community as well as to the laymen for frequent study and reflection. This inscription is important for questions related to the chronology of the Pali canon as it exists today. The passages referred to by Asoka have been identified with parts of works in the second division of the Pali *Tipitaka,* or Three Baskets. The Three Baskets contain collections of the Buddha's pronouncements on monastic discipline, his sermons and sayings, and exegetical literature dealing with Buddhist metaphysics and psychological ethics. The Pali-Buddhist tradition asserts that the major sermons and sayings of the Buddha, as well as the code of monastic discipline, were first collected soon after the Master's demise in 487-486 B.C. This tradition also claims that a work called *Points of Controversy* by Moggaliputta Tissa, the president of the third council held during the reign of Asoka, was compiled to refute various heretical opinions prevailing during the Asokan age. Inscriptions immediately following the Asokan age mention various divisions of the Pali canon and lead us to conclude that the canon had emerged, more or less in its present form, soon after 200 B.C. There was also a considerable growth in the commentatorial literature in Pali, and at least a beginning was made in the compilation of Buddhist works in Mixed Sanskrit. It is possible that many of the Scriptural works were committed to writing, and that Mahendra, Asoka's son, took some of these texts with him to Ceylon.

The subject of written texts leads us to a consideration of the scripts in use during the Asokan age. Asoka's inscriptions mainly use two scripts, the Kharoshti (a variant of the Aramic popularized by the Persians and written from right to left) and Brahmi. The Kharoshti is used exclusively in the northwestern areas, whereas Brahmi (written from left to right) is used in all the other inscriptions. The Brahmi script shows two major regional variations called the northern and the southern, but other minor and subregional variations can also be noticed within the two major groups. That the script is fully developed and has reached a stage of regional development is an indication that it was already old in the third century B.C. In fact, the knowledge of writing in India goes back to a period at least prior to the seventh century B.C. The *Jatakas* reveal that writing and written documents were common at the time Buddhism arose, and there is a mention of a guessing game played with one child outlining letters in the air to be guessed by another, which shows that the art of writing had spread even to juvenile practitioners. We have already referred to the keeping of accounts and the writing of royal writs described in the *Arthashastra* of Kautalya. The professional writer was a familiar figure and was employed by governments, and one Chapada is known as a scribe working for Asoka. It was once held that the art of writing was introduced into India, and that the Brahmi script was derived from the Phoenician. The discovery of the Indus Valley script and recent studies in the development of ancient Indian scripts show that such a view is no longer tenable. In the absence of a satisfactory decipherment of

the Indus script it is difficult to speak of positive interrelation-
ships between the Indus script and the Brahmi, though the possibility of the latter being derived, at least in part, from the former
cannot be absolutely ruled out.[18]

Besides the Buddhist literature in Pali there existed an extensive literature in Sanskrit. There were the three *Vedas* and the
Brahmanas, Aranyakas, and the *Upanishads* (the major ones),
which were certainly known at the time of the Buddha. Likewise,
the two epics must have been known in some form. Stories from
the *Ramayana* and the *Mahabharata* appear in varied forms in
the Pali *Jatakas.* Dramatic presentations were a prominent part
of the *Samajas,* and such presentations must have used some kinds
of "texts." Panini's grammar is generally recognized as a product
of about the fifth century B.C. The *Arthashastra* refers to a number of schools of political theorists, indicating the development of
the science of polity and literature bearing on it before the third
century B.C.[19] Besides the *Vedas,* Kautalya mentions phonetics,
ceremonial injunctions, grammar, glossorial explanation of ob-
scure Vedic terms, prosody, and astronomy as fit subjects for
study. The reference to the school of Manu would indicate the
existence of the *dharmashastra* school, as well as the heterodox
schools of philosophy like the Samkhya and the Lokayata. All of
these produced their own extensive literature, and hence the literary legacy for the Asokan age was both rich and extensive.

Still another class of literature available to the Asokan age was
that of the Jainas. Mahavira and the Buddha were contemporaries, and the development of the two creeds ran somewhat
along parallel lines. Asoka's reference to the *asinavas* (evil tendency of the mind) is taken by many scholars as closer to the Jain
concept than the Buddhist, and his belief in non-violence certainly shows Jainistic influences. Asoka urges reverence toward
the *Nigranthas* (Jain ascetics), and it is very probable that he was
familiar with the creed of the Jainas as preserved in their own
literature. The same may have been the case with the Ajivikas,
for whom Asoka provided cave dwellings as attested to by the
Barabar Hill Cave Inscriptions. As we saw at the outset of this
work, Pali tradition asserts that Asoka's mother was an adherent
of the Ajivika sect, and it would not be at all improbable that
Asoka gained acquaintance with their doctrines in his youth.

The age of Asoka, therefore, had a rich legacy in literature, which ranged from religious to secular poetry and dramatic representations, and was expressed in Sanskrit as well as the Prakrits of the time. Both as a prince and in his later royal career Asoka displayed an avid curiosity about doctrines and ideas and strove to know as much as he could about people, their faiths, and their notions. He was a man of exceptional cultural attainments and must have been a voracious "listener" if not a reader in his own right.

IV

The reign of Asoka was noteworthy in still another area of accomplishments. "The history of Buddhist art" writes J. Vogel, "does not really commence until the reign of the great Asoka, *circa* 250 B.C., two centuries and a quarter after Buddha's nirvana." [20] Pali tradition credits Asoka with having built thousands of stupas and monasteries, and though the number is an obvious and pious exaggeration, it does contain a core of truth. It seems probable that the second distribution of the relics of the Buddha's body took place during the reign of Asoka, and that the earliest stupa at Samchi may be attributed to the Asokan age.[21] Asoka himself states that he set up pillars at the holy places of Buddhism. It is not at all improbable that he also built monasteries for the Buddhist fraternity. All these activities involved extensive building and sculpturing operations, for which there is scarcely any parallel for a single lifetime.

The achievements of Asokan art can be assessed only against the background of pre-Mauryan art. The earliest examples of Indian art and architecture belong to the Indus civilization as represented in the ruins of Mohenjo Daro and Harappa, now in West Pakistan. The Indus art already shows a degree of sophistication, indicating a long tradition of plastic art, and the planning and construction of the city and its environs at Mohenjo Daro rightly evoke a sense of wonder and admiration. This civilization disappears from the surface of Indian life by 1500 B.C., and from that time up to about the third century B.C. there is a long gap in the history of art in India. The Vedic and post-Vedic architecture used wood and brick, and hence specimens of these ages have completely disappeared. Literary descriptions, however, give us some idea of the nature and layout of these towns and villages. The excavations at Pataliputra also convey

to us an idea of pre-Asokan monumental buildings. The Pali
texts indicate that the custom of erecting stupas was certainly
pre-Buddhist. When the Master was on his deathbed, his disciples
asked him about the disposal of his mortal remains. The Buddha
said that his body might be cremated and over the remains a
stupa might be built. It was, he added, the normal practice to
enshrine the funeral remains of a king or a great man. The practice of erecting such a funeral monument, then, was fairly common during the time of the Buddha. Such a practice, in fact, goes
back to the Vedic times, for among the methods of disposal of the
dead, the erection of funeral monuments over relics deposited in
an urn is clearly mentioned in Vedic literature. The *Mahapari-
nibbana sutta* tells us that the bodily remains of the Buddha, such
as bones and ashes, were divided into eight parts, and over these,
stupas were built at various places. These early stupas were hemispherical mounds of bricks and stones enshrining the relics deposited in an urn and buried in the body of the stupa. But,
whereas the earlier stupas were purely commemorative edifices,
the Buddhist stupas developed into places of devotion and worship when Buddhism grew into a religion. It was then considered
an act of merit to worship at the stupa, and hence certain struc-
tural changes were introduced to meet the new functional needs
of the stupa. The most important additions were the shaft surmounted by the "umbrella," which was a sign of power and authority; the circumambulatory path; places for the offering of
flowers and the placing of candles and incense sticks; and finally,
the erection of railings surrounding the stupa and opening into
four gateways facing each direction. These railings and gateways
were then covered with profuse sculptural illustrations from the
Jatakas, which contained episodes from the past lives of the Buddha and also the historical life of the Buddha. But the developments that led to profusely sculptured stone railings and gateways
appeared after the age of Asoka. The Asokan stupas were probably constructed from rubble masonry and were made in the form
of a hemispherical mound set on a platform with steps leading to
the base from each side. Nothing is known of their decorations, if
there were any, since the Asokan stupas were built over in later
ages.

The earliest excavated cave dwellings and shrines in India belong to the age of Asoka. Some seven of these monuments are

ascribed to the Maurya period. Of these, four are in the Barabar Hill and three in the Nagarjuni Hill, both of which are located in the Gaya district of Bihar. Of the Barabar cave temples, one Sudama (or Nyagrodha) was excavated in the twelfth year of Asoka's reign (257-256 B.C.), and the Gopi Cave belongs to the period of Asoka's grandson, Dasharatha. The Lomasa Rishi Cave is undated and unfinished and may belong to a period after Dasharatha. The Sudama or Asokan Cave consists of two apartments, of which the outer is rectangular and the inner circular. The two, though divided by a solid wall, are connected by a narrow passage. The outer chamber is covered by a barrel vault and the inner has a hemispherical dome. The sloping jambs of the doorway are clearly reminiscent of wooden prototypes. The Gopi Cave is forty-four feet long, nineteen feet wide, and ten feet high and has a vaulted roof. All of them have severely plain surfaces, though the interiors are highly polished "like glass." The Lomas Rishi Cave has a decorated frieze showing a row of elephants. Many of the elements of planning and architectural conventions found in these caves are later elaborated in the cave temples of western India.[22]

This architecture involved excavation of large masses of the hardest kind of rock with precision and deftness bespeaking experience in the art of stonecutting. Where did it originate? The idea of using caves and caverns as makeshift dwellings during the rainy season is mentioned in early Buddhist literature. If the use of natural caverns in the mountains was quite common in the days of the Buddha, it is only reasonable to assume that the idea of a cave shrine or dwelling was indigenous in origin when Asoka ordered his own cave dwellings for the Ajivikas. However, Sir John Marshall argues, "The practice of hollowing out chambers had been common in Egypt from time immemorial, and by the sixth century B.C., had spread as far east as Persia, where the royal tombs of Darius and his successors of the Achaemenian dynasty up to the time of Codomannus (335-330 B.C.) were excavated in the cliffs of Naksh-i-Rustam and Persepolis. From Persia the idea found its way during the third century before our era into Hindustan and resulted, as we have already seen, in the excavation of dwelling places and chapels for ascetics in the Barabar Hills and Bihar."[23] That there was Persian inspiration behind the sudden acquisition of skill in working in stone by the Asokan artist is an assumption that is reasonably supported by available evidence. But, as we have noted above, there is no need to go to Persia to search for the origin of the idea of using a cave as a dwelling or shrine in India. Furthermore, the copy of wooden prototypes in the sloping jambs is clear evidence of the transference of techniques of architecture in wood to stone by the Asokan artists. The only Persian influence that may be positively discerned is the high degree of polish given to the inner surfaces in these cave dwellings.

If the cave temples give an indication of the capabilities of the Asokan artists, the pillars are evidence of their great achievements. Asoka seems to have set up as many as thirty pillars at different spots in his empire; of these, ten have survived in more or less perfect state, and four exist in a damaged condition. They are monolithic and reflect as much engineering skill as great artistic achievement. They are all "monumental in conception and design, and inordinately fine, orderly, thorough and precise in execution." All of them, again, are executed in hard gray sandstone of large dimensions, very dextrously chiseled and given a lustrous polish, perhaps through an application of silicious varnish. The material for these huge columns seems to have been derived from a quarry at Chunar, in Bihar, where a great art center under the patronage of the Maurya court must have flourished. They range in height from thirty to forty feet, and the quarrying of the stones, their fabrication into highly polished columns, and transportation to distant places (some of them weighed over forty tons) were intricate technical problems that seem to have been solved with great skill.

A chronology of these columns on stylistic grounds has been attempted by Nihar Ranjan Ray. According to him, the earliest is one at Basarh-Bakhira, and it may have been pre-Mauryan. The Sankishya column comes next, belonging to the twelfth or thirteenth regnal year of Asoka. The Rampurva (bull) column may date from the same period followed by the Rampurva (lion) and Lauriya-Nandangarh (lion) columns. The latest ones are those at Sarnath and Samchi.[24] The columns at Delhi (Mirath and Topra), Allahabad, Lauriya-Araraj, Lauriya-Nandangarh, Rampurva (lion), Sankishya, Samchi, Rummindei, Nigali-Sagar, and Sarnath bear inscriptions, and the Rampurva (bull), Basarh-Bakhira, and Kosam have no edicts on them. The columns have a plain, smooth shaft, circular in section and slightly tapering appearance. This is surmounted by a capital, "arched bell," and formed of lotus petals joined to the shaft by a copper bolt of cylindrical shape bulging in the middle. The abacus is square and plain in the earlier types, changing to a circular and decorated form in later examples. Then comes the crowning part of animal figures in the round, forming a single piece with the abacus. These animals are shown either singly or in groups. The animals shown are the bull (Rampurva), lion (Rampurva), elephant (Sankishya), or four lions seated back to back (Sarnath), and horses and geese. There is also a representation of four semi-bulls seated back to back at Salempur in Mazuffarabad district in Bihar.

What is the origin of the idea of setting up such pillars? They may have been erected by Asoka to commemorate the various places of his pilgrimage. On the other hand, it is possible that some pillars were already in existence before the time of Asoka, and he simply inscribed his edicts on them. The custom of setting up pillars as lampposts (*dipasthambhas*) or flagpoles (*dhwajas-thambas*) was very ancient, and there is nothing extraordinary in such pillars being erected to commemorate holy spots. In his Rummindei Pillar Inscription Asoka clearly states that he set up the pillar (*silathabhe cha usapite*)[25] in his twentieth year at the birthplace of the Buddha, where he worshipped. Asoka also mentions in his Minor Rock Edict II that he ordered his rescripts to be inscribed on hill rocks and "wherever there is a stone pillar." It is quite clear, therefore, that the custom of setting up pillars, wood or stone, existed before Asoka's time, and he simply used this custom to bring into existence some of the finest examples of the Indian stonecutter's and sculptor's art.

These pillars reflect the essential personality of the great king and the ethos of his age. The vision that conceived them was imperial in intentions, and the art that executed them undoubtedly received, in part at least, its inspiration from outside the national and cultural frontiers of the country. Their polish reflects the elegance of the Maurya court; their loftiness is an index of the high soaring ambition of the dynasty; and their capitals, which have rarely been equaled in excellence, proclaim the piety of Asoka, the righteous.

The animals were selected with special care to underscore the twofold mystique of the emperor. Asoka was both an emperor and a pious Buddhist. We have already discussed his familiarity with the Buddhist literature of his times. It is not unreasonable, therefore, to hold that the symbolism used by him, by and large, came from the Buddhist imagery. We have mentioned that he used the symbols of lion, horse, bull, wheel, and geese on his monuments. Of these, the lion is well-known in similes in Pali literature. The lion is the king of the wilds, is without fear and dread, and when he roars all the other denizens of the jungle are silent. The Buddha's preaching is called the lion's roar; his way of sleeping is known as *sihaseyya,* or the lion's posture. He is also compared to the lone lion who is always watchful and diligent. The lion, therefore, in the Asokan symbolism, personifies both the glory of the Buddha and the majesty of the Maurya Empire.

The other symbols have equally Buddhist and imperial associations. The horse stands for the Buddha's renunciation and is used in later art as an indication of the Bodhisattva leaving his home. The strong disciplined horse is often employed as a comparison for a good man, and the training of a wise man is frequently compared to the training of a horse. The horse is also one of the famous seven jewels of a *Cakkavatti,* or a Universal Monarch. The Buddha is very often compared to an elephant in battle, and the White Elephant is used as a symbol of the conception of the Bodhisattva in Buddhist art. At Dhauli there is a most impressive representation of an elephant emerging from the rock. At Kalsi there is the well-drawn figure of an elephant with the phrase *gajatame,* or most excellent elephant. The elephant, thus, is simultaneously used as an emblem of the Buddha, so full of endurance, strength, restraint, and majesty as well as of the imperial grandeur of the Mauryas, for, like the horse, the miraculous elephant is also a part of the paraphernalia of the Universal Monarch. The bull stands for strength and productivity. The goose is a favorite motif of decoration in Indian art and frequently occurs in similes in Pali literature. The *hamsa,* wrongly translated as swan according to J. P. Vogel, is a bird of passage of marvelous origin; it has the ability of discrimination symbolized in its skill in separating water from milk; it has a graceful gait and charming voice and is remarkably loyal to its mate.[26] The Buddha is shown as being born, in one of his earlier lives, as the king of the geese. The goose, therefore, has a specific religious significance for a Buddhist.

It has been argued with much force that Asokan art shows two distinct traditions, one of which is purely indigenous, and the other deriving its inspiration from Medo-Achaemenian and Hellenistic cultures. To the former tradition belong the Dhauli elephant and the Rampurva bull. This art of sculpture in stone evolved from wooden prototypes, and its antiquity may even date back to the prehistoric ages of Indian history. The other school is represented by the lion, which was treated with extreme stylization, the essential conventions of which were already fixed and well-established in the Medo-Achaemenian and Hellenistic art traditions. To the artistic qualities of the Asokan monuments, Nihar Ranjan Ray pays a well-deserved tribute: "The total aesthetic effect of Maurya columns has never been surpassed in later Indian art and in the whole realm of independent monumental columns of the world Mauryan columns occupy a proud position by reason of their very free and significant artistic form in space, the rhythmic and balanced proportion of their constituent elements, the unitary and integrated effect of the whole, their chaste and elegant shaft and capital, and no less by the conscious, proud and dignified attitude of the crowning ornaments." [27]

Asokan art represents a significantly revolutionary phase in the art history of India. For the first time, perhaps, stone replaced wood for monumental sculpture, and the skill and grace with which the intractable material was handled show a mastery that is difficult to acquire in a single generation. It is suggested that there were three distinct groups involved in the fabrication of the monuments of the Asokan age. One was that of Indians working in the pure indigenous tradition, as revealed in the Sankishya elephant, the Dhauli elephant, and the Rampurva bull. The second group was that of Indians influenced by the west Asian art traditions, and the third was that of colonial artists of the Hellenistic Orient imported by the Maurya court. It is this combination that imparts to Asokan art an urban, conscious, and civilized quality, its advanced power of visualization and masterly comprehension of the third dimension. In some of the outstanding examples an exotic element has been seen, and it is attributed to the phil-Hellenism of the Maurya court. The Asokan monuments "reveal the same imperialist, and autocratic character of Asoka's rule in its essential structure; like so much of Maurya culture, they are foreign in style, quite apart from the main stream and tradition of Indian art and display the same intimacy of relationship and imitation of the cultures of the Hellenistic Western powers and of Iran as the language of Asoka's inscriptions and the Maurya court's phil-Hellenic leaning." [28] This was a court art *par excellence,* a grand effulgence of an imperial vision characterized by piety of thought, earnestness of intentions, and eclecticism in its technical choice. It was art as conceived by the great Asoka, and it reflected his personality to its fullest capacity. When he disappeared from the historical scene, the art too vanished, for Asokan art is an episode in the art history of India, a flower of a rare personal initiative and exotic nourishment.

Of the architectural remains of the Asokan age we have virtually nothing. The excavations at Pataliputra laid bare the imposing remains of the imperial palace, which, Ray argues, may have been built by Asoka himself "since their essential ideology and the conception agree so remarkably well with all that we already know of the aims, ideals, motives and general ideological design of that great benevolent autocrat." [29] It has also been suggested that the earliest stupa at Samchi may belong to the Asokan age, since it is known that the second distribution of the Buddha's relics took place during his reign. Asoka must have also built many monasteries for the use of the Buddhist fraternity of monks and nuns, but there is no trace left of these.

A brief reference may here be made to other artistic remains ascribed either to the Asokan age or to a period following it. Of the former a small rail at Sarnath and a throne in the inner temple at Bodhagaya are attributed to the Asokan age. Then there are the *Yaksha* figures from Patna, the statue of a *yakshi* from Didarganj, the over life-size statue from Parkham, the damaged Tirthamkara images from Lohanipur, and the torso of a *yaksha,* or a royal figure, from Baroda near Mathura, all of which are notable examples of early Indian art. The beautiful Didarganj *yakshi* figure is artistically the most outstanding among these examples. But many scholars have doubted that these figures could be ascribed to the Asokan age as they belong altogether to a different art tradition. This other tradition, however, was as much a part of Mauryan India as was the Perso-Hellenistic-inspired art of the Maurya court. A number of terra-cotta figurines of religious and secular import have been discovered from sites in northwestern and northern India, and they significantly show that this indigenous tradition of Mauryan India had a profound influence on the art of succeeding ages.[30]

Archaeological excavations at Kaushambi, Mathura, Taxila, Rajgir, Patna, Maheshwar, and many other places have revealed the existence of a great and flourishing tradition in pottery-making ascribed to the Maurya age. The most important of these categories of pottery is the ware described as the Northern Black Polished ware made of fine levigated clay with a brilliant polished glaze. Many examples of dishes and other small ware have been found at widely scattered sites indicating a brisk trade in this kind of pottery, which was valued both for its strength and fine polish. Available evidence suggests that a large manufacturing center of this ware existed in the Gangetic valley area, possibly in the neighborhood of Kaushambi. Other kinds of pottery were the black, gray, and red varieties displaying a well-developed technique of firing.[31] A large number of copper and silver punch-marked coins unearthed at various sites has been attributed to the Mauryan period. All such evidence speaks of a vigorous, fine, and utilitarian art tradition ushered in by the Maurya dynasty and finding fulfilment in the reign of Asoka.

VII

In the foregoing pages we have attempted a broad survey of the cultural conditions of the age of Asoka. This picture is one of apparent economic strength, peace, and security, brisk trade and commerce, and flourishing industries. It is also an age of great art traditions and the development of Pali literature enshrining the words of the Buddha. Much of this was in the making long before Asoka appeared on the scene, but he left the indelible mark of his remarkable personality on much. Of his intentions there could be little doubt. He attempted a vast transformation of society on two distinct levels. On the one hand, he inherited the primitive and tribal society of the past and strove to create out of it a unified and national society. On the other hand, he strove to remake this society into a united body infused with a sense of ethical purpose that would help its constituents transcend the barriers of region, tribe, caste, and class. On the political level, he earnestly endeavored to eschew war and formulate political relations in terms that were as new as they were revolutionary. In this respect, perhaps, Asoka stands alone among the galaxy of rulers of humanity, for there is no parallel where war was renounced by an empire of such vast dimensions. In the field of religion he took a struggling sect and transformed it into a great religion, destined to spread all over Asia and to usher in a millennium of great achievements in the cultural history of India. Asoka felt that Buddhism alone could help him replace tribalism with a new and universal philosophy of life based on man, rather than on men with all their divisions into castes, tribes, races, and creeds. Once he grasped this truth, as he understood it, he spent his whole life pursuing his ideal. It was during the time of his grandfather and of Asoka that the cultural isolation of India was shattered, for the Mauryas were not afraid of intercultural contacts and borrowing.

The Maurya rulers, and especially Asoka, were men confident of themselves and convinced of their mission of making a great age. They did not have to worry about the risks of borrowing from others. And Asoka's own confidence was further reinforced by his understanding of the universality of the Buddha's message and the culture created by it.

Was the reign of Asoka an unqualified success? Asoka ruled for some forty years, until *circa* 233-232 B.C. In less than half a century after his rule, by 186 B.C. (or 183 B.C.), his mighty empire crumbled. While reviewing his troops, the last of the Mauryas, Brihadratha, was assassinated by his Brahmin commander, Pushyamitra Shunga, the founder of the Shunga dynasty that ruled (until 75 B.C.) over what was left of the Asokan empire. It has been argued that Asoka must be held primarily responsible for the decline of the Mauryas. Some have described his religious policy as the major factor leading to the decline and downfall of the Maurya dynasty. But the disintegration of an empire is much too complex a process to be satisfactorily explained by the operation of single causes. Let us briefly discuss the many causes which led to the end of the Maurya dynasty.

The successors of Asoka (nine or seven in number) ruled over a period of less than half a century, each accounting for a span of time ranging between thirteen and seven years. Such uniformly short reigns cannot be described as normal and indicate serious disturbances of which history has left little or no record. These disturbances, among which may be listed possible disputed successions, must have damaged the structure of the empire to the extent that it needed only an act of assassination to topple it.

We may also consider the possibility of the dismemberment of the Maurya Empire soon after the death of Asoka. The Maurya bureaucracy, as pointed out previously, tended to be harsh and despotic. Asoka himself had to suppress a revolt in Taxila, where he was told by the people that they were not against the king but his tyrannical ministers. Jaluka, one of the sons of Asoka, is mentioned as having ruled only in Kashmir; and Simuka, the founder of the Satavahana dynasty, may have been an officer in the employ of the Mauryas in the Deccan. In this way parts of the empire tended to become independent either as a result of disunity in the ruling family or royal ambitions entertained by its powerful officers.

The economic consequence of imperial rule must not be ignored in considering the process of the decline of the Maurya Empire. The Mauryas maintained large armies and a numerous bureaucracy. These cost the exchequer a substantial part of its budget. To these must be added the cost of religious and monumental construction. Asoka built innumerable monasteries, the earliest stupa at Samchi and perhaps others at various places, and set up numerous pillars of impressive dimensions, all of which must have cost the imperial treasury substantial amounts of money. Asoka's policy of colonization through the forced settlement of war captives may indicate that the empire had reached its limit of expansion in the settled areas and thus had to find new areas. There is an indication of the debasement of currency between the reign of Chandragupta and that of Asoka. This debasement must be construed as a sign of an impending economic crisis, which reached destructive proportions after the death of Asoka. Also, we cannot rule out the possibility of social discontent. Asoka's prohibitory orders and regulatory commandments, although inspired by high ethical motives, must have interfered with the lives of the people. His numerous inspectors and agents, in their zealous activities, must have created resentment against an administration that had eyes and ears all over the land, that often became arbitrary and punitive, and taxed heavily rich and poor alike. Asoka advised his people to show respect to Brahmins and holy men of all sects, and he strove to be impartial in his patronage to religious establishments. But he also prohibited animal sacrifices, scoffed at popular religious rites and ceremonies, and claimed that he had mingled gods with men on this very earth. Some authorities have argued that a Brahmanical counter-revolution was mainly responsible for the downfall of the Mauryas, and though this may be an oversimplification, resentment of the Brahmanical leadership against the heterodox Mauryas may have played a part in creating sentiments of antipathy against Mauryan rule in the popular mind.

Then there were the foreign invasions. In the second century B.C. northern India was invaded by the Greeks, led by Demetrius and Menander. This invasion must have occurred within a few decades of the death of Asoka and must have led to the loss of the Punjab to the Maurya Empire. This Greek invasion must have hastened the process of disintegration.

Finally, there is something to be said about the average time-span of an empire in Indian history. There were four great empires in the long history of India. The Maurya Empire lasted for about 137 years. The Gupta Empire, which began its career in 320 A.D., was already in decline by 475 A.D. The Mughal Empire was really established only after 1560, and after 1707 its disintegration began. The British Empire crushed the last challenge to its establishment in 1818 and it was ended by 1947. Seen in this context, then, it seems that the average life-span of an Indian empire ranges between 125 to 160 years. Without necessarily subscribing to the organic or cyclical theories in historical interpretation, it seems clear that the life-span of the Maurya Empire was but a part of the general process of imperial expansion and disintegration as illustrated by the history of India.[32]

To what extent, then, should we hold Asoka personally responsible for the decline of the Maurya Empire? We must avoid the two extremes of holding him wholly responsible and acquitting him completely of the charge. It is possible to argue that Asoka's experiment in righteousness did disturb a delicate equilibrium of social forces, an equilibrium which was the basis of the imperial structure. He was far too otherworldly to arrest the onset of the process of disintegration, and his various policies must have had a disturbing effect on the balance of forces holding the empire together. In short, Asoka forgot or would not recognize that the way of empires and the path of righteousness were two entirely different undertakings, and this had inevitable consequences for his empire.

But in a sense the Asokan adventure was unique. His two great mentors were Kautalya and the Buddha. One interpreted the world purely in terms of political realism and *Machtpolitik*. The Buddha turned his back on the world of common human preoccupations with toil and strife and attempted his own interpretation of existence in ethical terms. It fell to Asoka to work out a viable synthesis of these two divergent philosophies of India, and the wonder is that he succeeded even for a short while. A universal ethical philosophy, an imperial vision, a realistic administrative ethos, and a paternalistic interest in the affairs of the subjects: these were the constituents of the Asokan world view. He had inherited a vast empire, and he proceeded to make it great in terms of enduring qualities. Such a great empire must bring into being a great cosmopolitan culture, and Asoka spent his years after the Kalinga war making this possible. Firm in determination, ceaseless in effort, pious in his thoughts, but imperious in his commands, Asoka stands towering far above the crowd of kings and princelings whose names and memories fill the Indian historical landscape.

Appendix

THE INSCRIPTIONS OF ASOKA

There are some thirty-three inscriptions of Asoka which are given
here in translation. Of these, twenty-two are on rocks and eleven
on pillars. Their locations, language, script, and content are discussed at appropriate places elsewhere in this work. The translation is based mainly on my own readings and a liberal use of the
emendations and comments of Hultzsch, Barua, Mookerji, and
Smith. The Kandahar Inscription in the Greco-Aramic versions is
based on the text and translation given by P. H. L. Eggermont
and J. Hoftijzer in *The Moral Edicts of King Asoka.*

I have attempted to be as literal as possible but have departed
from literal renderings wherever I felt sense and spirit of the text
could be better brought out for the non-specialist. I have left
Asoka's titles, *Devanampiya Piyadasi* (Beloved of the gods, of
Benevolent Mien) untranslated. Terms such as *dhammalipi* and
dhamma are rendered as rescript on morality and morality. Other
technical terms like *Mahamatra, Dharmamahamatra, Rajuka,
Purusha,* and *Parishad* are rendered in their broad and general
sense as high officials, morality officers, officers, agents, and council
respectively. These will not be satisfactory for the specialist, but I
hope the layman will find them adequate and convenient.

ROCK EDICTS

One

This rescript on morality has been commanded to be written by
the King Devanampiya Piyadasi. Here no animal may be slaughtered and offered in sacrifice. No convivial assembly too may be

held. For King Devanampiya Piyadasi sees many a blemish in convivial assemblies. But there are some assemblies considered good by King Devanampiya Piyadasi. Formerly in the kitchen of King Devanampiya Piyadasi every day hundreds of thousands of animals were slaughtered for curry. But now since this rescript on morality has been written only three animals are slaughtered for curry; two peacocks and one deer, and that deer too not always. Even these three animals will not be slaughtered hence.

Two

In all the dominions of King Devanampiya Piyadasi, even on the frontiers and in the territories of the Cholas, Pandiyas, Satiyaputra, Keralaputra, even up to Tambraparni, and in the domains of the Greek King Antiochus and his neighbors, everywhere King Devanampiya Piyadasi has arranged for two kinds of treatments, of men and animals. And those medicinal herbs that are beneficial to men and animals have been brought and planted wherever they did not exist. Roots and fruits too have been brought and planted wherever they did not exist. On the highways, wells have been dug, and trees planted for the use of men and animals.

Three

King Devanampiya Piyadasi says thus: Twelve years after my coronation have I ordered thus! Everywhere in my dominions, the officers (Yuktas, Rajukas and Pradeshikas) will embark on tours of inspection every five years for the inculcation of morality and other such works. (They will instruct my subjects that) obedience to father and mother is excellent, liberality to friends, acquaintances and kinsmen, to Brahmins and ascetics is excellent; excellent is abstention from the slaughter of animals; and abstemiousness and few possessions are excellent. The council (Parishad) will also order the officers (Yuktas) to enforce these, both in their letter and spirit.

Four

For a long time in the past, for many hundreds of years have increased the sacrificial slaughter of animals, violence toward creatures, unfilial conduct toward kinsmen, improper conduct toward Brahmins and ascetics. Now with the practice of morality by King Devanampiya Piyadasi, the sound of war drums has become the call to morality. As has not come to pass for many hundreds of years, through the rescript on morality, issued by King Devanampiya Piyadasi, and by the exhibition of (edifying spectacles such as) heavenly mansions, elephants, columns of fire and other heavenly forms, all this has increased namely, non-slaughter of animals for sacrificial purposes, non-violence toward beings, proper attention to kinsmen, proper attention to Brahmins and ascetics, welfare of mother and father, welfare of the aged and many other kinds of moral behavior; all these have increased. This shall increase further. And the sons, grandsons and great grandsons of King Devanampiya Piyadasi will further the practice of morality, until the very end of the universe, by standing firm in morality and character and will instruct therein. That indeed is the best of deeds namely, inculcation of morality. For those lacking in character, practice of morality is not possible. Hence good, verily, is the furtherance of morality and decrease in immorality. For this purpose this has been commanded to be written that everyone shall exert for the progress of morality and not for its decrease. This has been commanded to be written by King Devanampiya Piyadasi since he was crowned twelve years ago.

Five

King Devanampiya Piyadasi says thus: Benevolence is difficult; he who performs a benevolent act accomplishes something difficult. I have performed much that is benevolent. Benevolence shall also be practiced by my sons, grandsons and their descendants even until the very dissolution of the universe. But he who neglects even a part hereof does evil. To commit sin, indeed, is easy.

In times past, formerly, there were no morality officers (Dharmamahamatras). Since I have been crowned thirteen years ago, I have appointed morality officers. They are engaged with votaries of all faiths, for the firm establishment of morality, for its progress, for the happiness here and hereafter of those devoted to morality. They are employed among the Greeks, Kambojas, Gandharas, Rashtrikas, Petenikas and among the frontier peoples.

They are employed among the servants and masters, among Brahmins, the destitute and the aged, for their benefit and happiness, for the removal of hindrances for those devoted to morality. They are engaged in helping those incarcerated, in preventing harassment and securing release of those who have large families or have been overwhelmed with calamity or are old. Here in Pataliputra or elsewhere they are employed in all towns, in all the harems of my brothers and establishments of my sisters and other kinsmen. They are employed among all those who are devoted to morality or are established therein everywhere in my dominions. For this purpose has this rescript on morality been written that it may long endure and that my subjects may practice it.

Six

King Devanamapiya Piyadasi says thus: For a long time past (proper arrangements for) the speedy dispatch of business and reporting at all times did not exist. That I have done. At all times, whether I am eating, or in the women's apartments, or in the inner chambers, in the cattle-pen or riding, or in the garden, everywhere reporters are posted so that they may inform me of the people's business. Everywhere I transact the people's business. Whatever I command orally, whether it concerns a gift or proclamation, or whatever that is entrusted to the officers, or whenever there is an urgent matter in dispute or deliberation in the Council, the matter may be reported to me speedily in all places and times. This I have commanded. I am never too satisfied with exertion or dispatch of business. For I regard the welfare of the people as my chief duty. The basis of that is exertion and proper dispatch of public business. There is no other work more important (for me) than the welfare of all people. And why? For the discharge of my debt to the people, so that I may give happiness to some here and win heaven hereafter. For this purpose this rescript on morality has been written, that it may last long, that my sons, grandsons and great grandsons may exert for the welfare of the entire world. This is most difficult of accomplishment except through strenuous effort.

Seven

King Devanampiya Piyadasi desires that all sects may live every-where. All of them desire restraint and purity of the mind. But men are of diverse desires and passions. They will practice all (points of their faith) or only a part. Even for a generous man, if he not have restraint, purity of mind, gratefulness or steadfastness in faith, there is no greatness.

Eight

For a long time past kings used to go on pleasure tours, such as hunting, and other amusements. But since he was crowned ten years ago King Devanampiya Piyadasi went on a pilgrimage of (the place of) Enlightenment of the Lord. Therein his tour of piety comprised visits to Brahmins and ascetics, charity and visits to the Elders (of the Buddhist Order) and gift of gold and visit to the country folk, instruction in the law of morality and inquiries pertaining thereto. The pleasure thereof is, indeed, great, exceeding any other.

Nine

King Devanampiya Piyadasi says thus: People perform many and diverse propitious ceremonies. In sickness, or marriage of sons and daughters, or for the gift of a son, or for (safety in) journey, in these and other matters, people perform diverse propitious ceremonies. And in this wives and mothers particularly indulge in ceremonies that are useless and empty. But ceremonies should be performed. But such ceremonies are of little value. But that indeed is a very valuable ceremony namely the ceremony (in behalf) of morality. It comprises proper treatment of slaves and servants, respect toward teachers, restraint (non-injury) toward living beings, gifts to Brahmins and ascetics, these and many such others are the ceremony of morality. Now, therefore, this should be said by a father, or son, or master, or husband, friend or acquaintance, or a neighbor. This is good; this is the kind of ceremony that should be performed for (the accomplishment of the proper) purpose.

And this too has been said: Charity is good. There is no

(greater) charity or favor than the gift of morality or favor of morality. And in this an acquaintance or friend, or kinsman or companion should instruct: This should be done; this is good. By this heaven may be gained. What more is worthy of performance for the accomplishment of heaven than this?

Ten

King Devanampiya Piyadasi does not think glory or renown great but the renown or glory he may acquire if the people harken to and act upon the Law of Morality he has enjoined. For this alone King Devanampiya Piyadasi wishes for glory and renown. Whatever exertion King Devanampiya Piyadasi undertakes, it is solely for the hereafter. And what is that? That all may be without blemish. Blemish is sin. That indeed is difficult of accomplishment by high or low except through the highest exertion and renunciation of all possessions. But this, indeed, is most difficult for one of high rank.

Eleven

King Devanampiya Piyadasi says thus: There is no gift like the gift of morality, praise of morality, sharing of morality or kinship with morality. It comprises proper treatment of slaves and servants, proper support of mother and father, liberality to friends, relations and kinsmen, Brahmins and ascetics, non-slaughter of beings. This should be addressed by a father to the son, brother, or friend, relation or kinsman, or even by a neighbor: This is good; this should be done. Acting thus he secures this world and the next and acquires infinite merit by that gift of morality.

Twelve

King Devanampiya Piyadasi honors all sectaries and those who have renounced household life as well as householders, with liberality and honors of various kinds. But King Devanampiya Piyadasi does not value gifts or honor for themselves. Why? For (he desires that) there should be the growth of the essential (spirit of morality or holiness) among all sects. That essential (spirit of morality or holiness) is of many kinds. But the root of that is restraint in speech. Why? That there should not be glorification of one's own sect and denunciation of the sect of others for little or no reason. For all sects are worthy of reverence for one reason or another. Acting thus one helps grow one's own sect and does good to the other's sect. Acting otherwise he belittles his own sect and does ill to the sect of another. He who glorifies his own sect and denounces the sect of another does so because of (excessive) love for his own sect. And why? (Thinking that) his own sect may shine (brighter). Acting thus, however, he harms his own sect. Harmony is good. Why? That people may listen to (the exposition of) each other's doctrine. This is the wish of King Devanampiya Piyadasi. What is it? All sectaries may be learned in the lore of another and fare well on the benevolent path. Those who are pleased with this should speak thus. King Devanampiya considers no liberality or honor greater than the growth of (the essential spirit of morality or holiness) of all sects. For this purpose are the morality officers and officers in charge of women and herdsmen and other groups, engaged. And this is its fruit that one's sect is advanced and morality (truth) is illumined.

Thirteen

Eight years after his coronation King Devanampiya Piyadasi conquered the Kalingas. In that (conquest) one hundred and fifty thousand people were deported (as prisoners), one hundred thousand were killed (or maimed) and many times that number died. Thereafter, with the conquest of Kalinga, King Devanampiya Piyadasi (adopted) the practice of morality, love of morality and inculcation of morality. For there arose in King Devanampiya Piyadasi remorse for the conquest of Kalinga. For when an unsubdued country is conquered there occur such things as slaughter, death and deportation of people and these are regarded as very painful and serious by King Devanampiya Piyadasi. Brahmins and ascetics live everywhere, as well as votaries of other sects and householders who practice such virtues as support of mother and father, service of elders, proper treatment of friends, relatives, acquaintances and kinsmen and slaves and servants and steadfastness in devotion to duties. They too suffer injury (separation from loved ones), slaughter and deportation of loved ones. And for those whose love is undiminished, their friends, acquaintances, relatives and kinsmen suffer calamity. And that is injury to them. This plight of men is regarded as serious by King Devanampiya Piyadasi. Outside of the territory of the Greeks there is no land where communities such as those of Brahmins and ascetics are not to be found. Nor is there any land where men do not have faith (religion) of one sect or another.

Hence, whatever the number of men then killed (or wounded) and died and were deported at the annexation of Kalinga, a hundredth or a thousandth part (thereof) even is regarded as serious by King Devanampiya Piyadasi. Furthermore, if anyone does wrong (to him) the person should be suffered or pardoned. To the forest folk, who live in the royal dominions of King Devanampiya Piyadasi, it may be pointed out that the king, remorseful as he is, has the strength to punish the wrongdoers who do not repent. For King Devanampiya desires that all beings should be safe, self-restrained, tranquil in thought and gentle.

King Devanampiya considers the victory of morality as the greatest. And this victory has been accomplished by King Devanampiya up to all his frontiers, even to a distance of six hundred *yojanas* where the Greek King Antiochus rules, and beyond Antiochus' realm in the dominions of the four kings called Ptolemy, Antigonas, Magus, and Alexander, downwards into the dominions of the Cholas and Pandyas, even up to Tamraparni. Similarly in the royal domains where live the Greeks, the Kambojas, Nabhakas, Nabhapantis, Bhojas, Pitinikas, Andhras and Paridas, everywhere people follow the instruction in morality by King Devanampiya. And wherever the ambassadors of King Devanampiya have fared there, too, people hear of his moral acts, his teachings and instruction on morality, and they follow morality and will do so.

Whatever has been gained by this victory of morality, that has been pleasant. This happiness has been secured through victory of morality but even that is not as great for the King Devanampiya as the gain of the next world. For this purpose this rescript on morality has been written that my sons and great grandsons should cease to think of new conquests and in all the victories they may gain they should be content with forbearance and slight punishment. For them the true conquest should be that of morality; all their delight should be delight in morality for benefit in this world and the next.

Fourteen

This rescript on morality has been commanded to be written by King Devanampiya Piyadasi. Some of it is short, some medium-length and other extensive. Everything has not been given everywhere. For my dominions are large wherein much has been commanded to be written and will be written. But some has been repeated again and again for its very sweetness, for the people to follow it. In some places it may be incorrectly written because of incompleteness, for want of space, or of damage to stone, or error of the scribe.

SEPARATE ROCK EDICT

One

By the command of Devanampiya the Princes and high officers of Tosali (or Samapa) are to be addressed thus: Whatever I perceive, that I desire to be put into practice by appropriate means. In this I hold my instructions to you to be the principal instrument for you are appointed (to rule) over thousands of human beings in the expectation that you will win the affection of all men. All men are my children. Just as I desire that my children will fare well and be happy in this world and the next, I desire the same for all men. You may not comprehend what all this means. Some individuals may understand this but some may understand it only in part and not entirely. You must ensure this that this policy is well carried out. There may be some who may suffer imprisonment or torture and in some cases there may be imprisonment without due process causing suffering and grief. In this you must follow a course of moderation (or impartiality) in justice. But there may not be success because of certain mental blemishes such as envy, loss (of mental equipoise), harshness, impatience, lack of application, sloth and weariness. But you must ensure that you do not display these blemishes. The basis of the whole matter lies in preventing the absence of loss (of mental equipoise) and haste in the implementation of principles (of justice). He who is slothful is not likely to exert himself. But you must act, move ahead, in your official duties. You must ensure this. And for this you must be told: Discharge the debt, in this wise, Devanampiya advises. Compliance with these instructions will be very fruitful; non-compliance, harmful. Non-compliance will secure neither the next world nor the service of the king. And why do I emphasize this so much? For your compliance will win you the next world and you will discharge your debt to me.

This proclamation must be made on the Tishya constellation days and in the interval between the Tishya days, and may be read aloud even to a single person. Acting in this wise you will obey my instructions. This Edict has been inscribed for this purpose that the town officers may exert themselves always, that none is imprisoned or tortured without due process. To ensure this I shall dispatch the high officers (Mahamatras) on quinquennial tours of inspection, who are not harsh or wrathful and are efficient and honest in their acts for they will know my intents and act accordingly. The Prince at Ujjayini, however, shall send out similar inspecting teams every three years. This holds true for Takshashila too. The high officers on their tours of duty will perform their functions in the awareness of my instructions.

SEPARATE ROCK EDICT

Two

By the command of Devanampiya the princes and high officers who are city-administrators of Tosali (and Samapa) are to be instructed thus: Whatever I perceive that I desire to be practiced by appropriate means. In this I hold my instructions to you to be the principal instrument. You are appointed (to rule) over thousands of human beings in the expectation that you will win the affection of all men. All men are my children. Just as I desire that my children will fare well and be happy in this world and the next I desire the same for all men. The unsubdued frontier peoples may wonder what the king designs for them. But my desire toward them is that they should understand that the king will forgive them as far as it is possible to forgive. For my sake they should practice the Law of Morality and win this world and next. For this I instruct you thus. This is the way to make you understand my will, my resolve and promise and discharge my debt to the people. Thus you should act. The people must be assured so that they may think that the king is to us even as a father, he feels for us even as he feels for himself for we are to him even as his children. My resolve is firm and so is my promise and I command unto you my will and my instructions. My messengers and special officers will be in contact with you. For you are capable of assuring the frontier peoples and ensure their welfare in this world and next. Acting thus you will gain the next world and discharge your debt to me. For this purpose has this Edict commanded to be written, that my high officers may engage themselves, for all future, in inspiring the frontier peoples and making them advance in the Law of Morality. This should be proclaimed by recitation on the Tishya day in all seasons and months, and also in the intervals. On special occasions it may be recited even to one person. Acting in this wise you will comply with my instructions.

MINOR ROCK EDICTS

Part One

From Suvarnagiri, by the order of the Prince and high officers, the high officers of Isila are to be wished well and addressed as follows: (The Rupnath Version has Devanampiya commands thus) For more than two and one-half years since I have been a lay-devotee I have not been exerting myself energetically. But for over a year since I approached the Order I have been exerting myself strenuously. In this time men who were separate from the gods in Jambudvipa have now mingled with them. This, verily, is the result of exertion. And this may be accomplished not by the great alone. For even a smaller man through his exertion can accomplish the great heaven. For this purpose this message is proclaimed that the great and small alike may exert themselves; that even the frontier peoples may know about it and such great exertion may long endure. This will increase and further increase, at least one and one-half times.

And for this purpose this must be written on rocks (or pillars). This must be spread all over your jurisdiction. This proclamation I have made while on a tour for 256 nights.

Part Two

Devanampiya says this: Mother and Father must be shown due respect; likewise the elders; proper regard for living beings must be firmly established, truth must be spoken. These values of morality must be propounded: Pupils must honor teachers; kinsmen must be well regarded. This is the ancient law, of long duration; this must be practiced. Written by the scribe Chapada.

BAIRAT (Bhabru) STONE INSCRIPTION

Piyadasi, the Magadhan King salutes the order and wishes them good health and comfort.

Sirs you are aware of my reverence and faith in the Buddha, the Dhamma and the Samgha. Whatever has been said by the Lord Buddha has been well said. However, reverend sirs, it occurs to me that the good doctrine may long endure, the following passages of the good doctrine may be especially pointed out, to wit: The Vinaya glorified; the powers of the elect; the dangers of the unknown; the song of the sage; the discourse on seclusion; the questions of Upatishya; the advice to Rahula on falsehood spoken by the Lord Buddha. I desire that many monks and nuns may listen to and meditate upon these; and so should the male and female lay-devotees. For this purpose, Sirs, I cause this to be written in order that people may know my wishes.

BARABAR HILL CAVE INSCRIPTIONS

Since he was crowned twelve years ago, King Piyadasi gave this Banyan Cave to the Ajivikas.

Since he was crowned twelve years ago King Piyadasi gave this cave in the Khalatika mountain to the Ajivikas.

Since he was crowned nineteen years ago King Piyadasi (declares): "I have given this cave in the very pleasant Khalatika mountain."

SAMCHI-SARNATH-KAUSHAMBI EDICT

To the high officials (of Pataliputra and Kaushambi) This is the command of King Devanampiya Piyadasi: "I have united the order. No one, monk or nun, shall split the order. Whosoever, monk or nun, causes a schism in the order shall be made to wear the white garments and expelled from the community." This command should be proclaimed to the order of the monks and nuns. King Devanampiya Piyadasi says this: Such an order must be posted on the highways within your jurisdiction. A copy of this should be made available to the lay-devotees. On the fasting days the lay-devotees should familiarize themselves with this order. Within your jurisdiction you should expel the schismatic. Similarly you must ensure the expulsion of the schismatic in all forts and districts in accordance with this command.

It is my desire that during the times of my sons and great grandsons, even so long as the sun and the moon endure, the Order may live completely united.

THE KANDAHAR INSCRIPTION

Greek Version

Ten years after his coronation King Piodasses instructed the people in morality. After that he made the people practice morality more and more.

There is prosperity in all the world.

The king refrains from violence to living beings as do the others and even the hunters and fishermen refrain from killing.

Those that were unrestrained have practiced restraint as much as it was possible for them to do.

Obedience to father and mother and elders has in the past led to a better life and will do so in future with the practice of the rules given above.

Aramic Version

Ten years after his coronation the King Piyadasi began to follow the true pattern of life. After that evil decreased for all men and misfortune disappeared due to the exertion of the king.

There were peace and happiness all over the earth. And this also happened namely, the few animals that were slaughtered for royal food have not been slaughtered and even the fishermen have been commanded to desist from fishing.

Those who were unrestrained now practice restraint. There is obedience to father and mother and elders as ordained and all those devoted to morality live confidently.

All of this has benefitted all men and will do so in future.

RUMMINDEI PILLAR INSCRIPTION

Here worshipped King Devanampiya Piyadasi when he was crowned twenty years ago, for here was born the Buddha, the sage of the Shakyas. A figure (of an elephant or "created a strong desire") and a stone pillar were set up. And because the Blessed one was born here, the village of Lumbini was exempted from taxes and made liable to pay only one-eight (or "made it a partaker of prosperity").

NIGALI SAGER PILLAR INSCRIPTION

Since he was crowned fourteen years ago King Devanampiya Piyadasi enlarged the Stupa of the former Buddha Konagamana, for the second time. And after twenty years since he was crowned he came here in person to offer worship and set up a stone pillar.

QUEEN'S EDICT

By the command of King Devanampiya Piyadasi, the high officials everywhere are to be addressed thus: Whatever gift is given by the Second Queen, to wit: mango-grove, garden or alms house or any other is to be regarded as her gift. These must be reckoned as the gifts of the second queen Kuruvaki, the mother of Tivara.

PILLAR EDICTS

One

King Devanampiya Piyadasi says thus: This rescript on morality has been commanded to be written by me since I was crowned twenty-six years ago. Happiness in this world and the next is difficult to achieve except through utmost devotion to morality, keen introspection, complete obedience, fear of evil and great exertion. Now because of my instruction this reliance on morality and devotion to it have increased daily and will increase. My officers, too, whether of the highest, middling or low ranks, must follow my instruction and practice it so that they may encourage the weak or hesitant as much as they can. Similarly the high officers (Mahamatras) of the frontiers must act. And this should be the norm of conduct that administration must confirm to morality, that legislation should be according to morality; this alone can make people happy according to morality and protect them according to the law of morality.

Two

King Devanampiya Piyadasi says thus: Morality is good. But what is morality? Few blemishes, much merit; compassion, liberality, truth and purity. Of my gifts there are many kinds for I have given the gift of eyes (truth) and I have conferred many benefits on bipeds and quadrupeds alike, even unto birds and creatures that live in the waters even to the extent of the gift of life. And I have done benevolent deeds of many other kinds. For this purpose this rescript on morality is commanded to be written, that it may be acted upon and may last long. He who accomplished this does good.

Three

King Devanampiya Piyadasi says thus: One sees only good actions; I have done this good deed. One does not see evil; I have done this evil or that this is a blemish. These are difficult to notice. But one should see this that anger, ruthlessness, wrath, pride, envy, all these result in evil. May these not cause my degradation. And this must be seen especially: this is beneficial to me in this world and the next.

Four

King Devanampiya Piyadasi says thus: Since I was crowned twenty-six years ago I have commanded this rescript on morality to be written. My officers (Rajukas) are appointed (to rule) over many hundreds of thousands of people. I have given them freedom in judging cases or inflicting punishments. Why? Because the officers (Rajukas) must function fearlessly and confidently and strive to ensure the benefit and happiness of (urban) people and the country folk. That they shall show favor to people and comprehend what causes happiness or suffering to them. And they shall instruct the (urban) people and the country folk in the principles of morality so that a beneficial here and hereafter may be ensured. The officers (Rajukas) are keen on serving me and will instruct the agents (Purushas) about my intentions. And they shall inform the officers about the ways in which the officers may act to please me. For even as a man who has given over his child to the care of a skilful nurse says, "the skilful nurse is energetic enough to look after my child's happiness"; so the officers have been appointed to ensure the benefit and happiness of the country folk in the expectation that they may perform their functions fearlessly, confidently, quietly and without distraction. For this I have granted my officers freedom in judging cases or inflicting punishments.

This much is desirable. And what is that? Equality in judicial procedure and equality in penalties. And henceforth this is my rule that to those in prison, condemned to death, a grace of three days has been granted by me. For during this time their kinsmen will urge them (Rajukas?) to ponder (to review the case) over the possibility of sparing their life or in case there is none to do this, then to meditate, give charity or perform acts of fasting for the next life. For this is my desire that even in this short time they may serve the next world and that among people the practice of morality of various kinds may grow, to wit self-restraint and distribution of charity.

Five

King Devanampiya Piyadasi says thus: Since I was crowned twenty-six years ago, I have made inviolate these species (of animals and birds) to wit; parrots, starlings, arunas, Brahmany ducks, wild geese, *nandimukhas, gelatas,* bats, queen ants, terrapins, boneless fish, *vedaveyakas, gangapuputakas,* skate, turtles, squirrels, Borasing stags, Brahmany bulls, rhinoceros, white pigeons, common pigeons, all quadrupeds that are not in use or are not eaten. Similarly she-goats, ewes, and sows whether young or milch, are inviolable; also young ones within six months of age are not to be killed. Cocks must not be caponed. Husks with living beings in them must not be burnt. Forests must not be burnt just for mischief or to destroy living beings in them. Life must not be fed on life. On the three seasonal full moon days and on full moon days of the month of Tishya for three days in each instance, to wit, the fourteenth and fifteenth days of the first half of the lunar month and the first day of the second half of the lunar month, as well as on fast days through the whole year, fish must not be killed or sold. During these days in the elephant-forests or fish-ponds no other species of animals must be destroyed.

On the eighth day, the fourteenth day and the fifteenth day in each fortnight as well as on the Tishya and Punarvasu days, no bulls must be castrated nor must goats, rams, boars or other animals be castrated.

On the Tishya and Punarvasu days, on the seasonal full-moon days and during the fort-night of the seasonal full-moons, horses and kine must not be branded. Since I was crowned twenty-six years ago I have granted twenty-five jail deliveries.

Six

King Devanampiya Piyadasi says thus: Since I was crowned twenty-two years ago I have commanded rescripts on morality to be written for the benefit and happiness of the world, so that the giving up of old ways may lead to advance in morality. This do I desire; the benefit and happiness of the world. To wit, I may accomplish the happiness and welfare of some of my relatives and persons near and far for which I may provide accordingly. In the same manner I regard all communities. I have honored all sects by diverse acts of worship. But this is the chief thing namely, personal attention to the needs of the people. Since I was crowned twenty-six years ago I have commanded this rescript on morality to be written.

Seven

King Devanampiya Piyadasi says thus: In times past Kings used to desire thus: How shall we make the people progress in morality? But the people did not progress appropriately in morality. In this King Devanampiya Piyadasi says thus: This occurred to me. In times past kings desired thus: How shall we make the people progress in morality? But the people did not progress appropriately in morality.

But how may the people be encouraged to act so that they may progress in morality? In what way can I help at least some of them to progress in morality? In this King Devanampiya Piyadasi says thus: This occurred to me. I shall cause the proclamation of morality to be proclaimed; I shall cause instruction in morality to be given. So that people may practice it and will advance themselves in it and thus will grow mightily the law of morality.

For this purpose proclamations on morality have been made, instructions of diverse kinds in morality commanded; so that my agents (Purushas) appointed to rule a multitude of people may expound and expand my teachings. My officers (Rajukas), too, set over many hundreds of thousands of men, have also been commanded by me thus: Instruct in this and thus the people (will be) "devoted to morality."

King Devanampiya Piyadasi says thus: With this very intention have I set up monuments to morality, appointed morality officers and caused proclamations of morality.

King Devanampiya Piyadasi says thus: On the highways Banyan trees have been planted so that they may afford shade to men and animals; mango-groves have been planted; wells have been dug at an interval of every half a *kos;* resting places have been set up; watering-places have been established for the benefit of animals and men. But the joy thereof has been slight indeed. In many ways kings in the past as well as I have attempted to comfort the world. I have done this in the desire that they may practice morality.

King Devanampiya Piyadasi says thus: My morality officers have engaged themselves in acts of royal benevolence in diverse ways. They are engaged among those that have renounced the world as well as the householders and among all sects. I have ordered them to be engaged in the welfare of the (Buddhist) Order as also the welfare of Brahmins, Ajivikas, Nigranthas and other sects.

These high officers will engage themselves in their diverse and respective duties whereas the morality officers are engaged specifically among all denominations in addition to other duties.

King Devanampiya Piyadasi says thus: These and many other officers are engaged in distribution of royal charity, on my account as well as on the Queen's account, and in all the royal households here and in the provinces; as also in dispensing charity on behalf of my sons and other princes so as to promote meritorious acts and encourage practice of morality; so that compassion, generosity, truth, mindfulness, gentleness and goodness will progress among mankind.

King Devanampiya Piyadasi says thus: Whatever good I have done has indeed been accomplished for the progress and welfare of the world. By these shall grow virtues namely: proper support of mother and father, regard for preceptors and elders, proper treatment of Brahmins and ascetics, of the poor and the destitute, slaves and servants.

King Devanampiya Piyadasi says thus: Men have been enabled to progress in morality by two means namely; by moral regulations and persuasion. But regulations are of little effect whereas persuasion is of higher efficacy.

I have made diverse moral regulations such as declaring classes of beings inviolate and many other kinds of moral regulations have I promulgated. By persuasion I have accomplished the growth of morality among men, through non-violence and non-slaughter of creatures. That has been done for this purpose namely, in the time of my sons and grandsons, even until the sun and moon endure, this shall be practiced. Doing this, this world and the next may be secured. Since I was crowned twenty-seven years ago, have I commanded this rescript on morality to be written.

King Devanampiya Piyadasi says thus: Wherever there are stone pillars or slabs there these rescripts on morality must be inscribed so that it may long endure.

Notes

The present work is based largely on materials drawn from inscriptions of Asoka and his age, and on literature in Pali and Sanskrit. Asoka's inscriptions are found in widely separated areas of India and Pakistan. The Rock Edicts are found at Sahahbazgarhi (in the Yusufzai subdivision of the Peshwar district in West Pakistan), Mansehra (in the Hazara district, also in West Pakistan), Girnar (near the town of Junagadh in Saurashtra in Gujarat State), a fragment at Sopara (near Bombay in Maharashtra), at Dhauli and Jaugada (in the Puri and Ganjam districts of Orissa) where the Two Separate Rock Edicts also have been found, Yerragudi (in the Kurnool district of Andhra Pradesh) and at Kalsi (in the Dehra Dun district of the state of Uttar Pradesh). The Pillar Inscriptions are located at Delhi (one pillar originally found at Topra in the Ambala district of East Punjab and the other at Meerut in Uttar Pradesh, where they were transported by Sultan Firozeshah Tughlag [1351-1388] in the fourteenth century A.D.), at Allahabad (where it was removed from Kosam in Uttar Pradesh), and at Radhia, Madhia and Rampurwa (all three places are in the Champaran District of Bihar). Only the Topra Pillar contains all seven edicts; the others have just the first six. Likewise the Minor Rock Edicts I and II are found in two general versions, northern and southern, and were located at Sahasram in South Bihar, Rupnath and Gujarra in the Jabalpur and Datia districts of the state of Madhya Pradesh, at Bairat in the state of Rajasthan, at Brahmagiri, Siddapura, and Jatinga-Rameshware in the Chitaldurg district in Mysore, and at Maski Govimath and Palkigundu, Yerragudi and Rajula-Mandagiri in the Raichur and Kurnool districts of Andhra Pradesh and at Bhabra in the Jaipur district of Rajasthan. The Minor Pillar Edicts were found at Sarnath (near Banaras in Uttar Pradesh), at Kaushambi (which also has the Queen's Edict), on the Allahabad Pillar mentioned above, and at Samchi in Madhya Pradesh. In the Nepalese Tarai were found the two commemorative pillars, one at Rummindei (where the Buddha was born) and at Nigliva. The Barbar caves (north of Gaya in South Bihar) have three Asokan and a few other inscriptions of the period inscribed on the walls.

An Asokan inscription in Greek and Aramaic was found in Kandahar in Afghanistan. It deals in general terms with the king's piety, and the measures taken by him to promote it. (Eggermont and Hoftijzer, *The Moral Edicts of Asoka*, pp. 42-45.) A copy of the *MRE*, I in its Sahasram version was discovered inscribed on two flat tops of a hillock called Bhandaridevi Hill in the village of Ahraura in Mirzapur district of the state of Uttar Pradesh. (For details see S. Sankarnarayan, "Ahraura Inscription of Asoka," *I.HQ*, XXXVII, 4,

December 1961, pp. 217-223.) Recently a bowl of gray schist with a major part of the seventh Rock Edict inscribed in the Kharoshti script was discovered in a curio shop in Bombay. The inscription is now in the Prince of Wales Museum of Bombay. Two edicts relating to grain storehouses and famine relief measures and ascribed to the Mauryas have also been found at Sohgura (Gorakhpur district in Uttar Pradesh) and Mahasthan (Bogra district in East Pakistan).

The author holds that the Buddhist literature in Pali and Mixed Sanskrit preserves, in a large measure, a genuine historical tradition concerning the life and activities of Asoka. He has, therefore, drawn on the canonical and non-canonical literature in Pali, the *Divyavadana*, the *Puranas*, the drama *Mudrarakshasa*, and the *Arthashastra* of Kautalya, which is now generally accepted, at least in its essentials, as a work of the Mauryan age. A great deal of literature on Asoka and his time based on modern research by Indian and Western scholars has grown through the past sixty years and the author has drawn freely on these scholarly labors. The bibliography gives details of the volumes used for the present study.

The following abbreviations are used:

AIU.   R. C. Majumdar and A. D. Pusalkar (eds.), *History and Culture of the Indian People, The Age of Imperial Unity.*
AngN.   *Anguttara Nikaya.*
Artha.   *Arthashastra.*
CHI.   E. J. Rapson (ed.), *Cambridge History of India.*
Dhp.   *Dhammapada.*
Divya.   *Divyavadana.*
DN.   *Digha Nikaya.*
IC.   *Indian Culture.*
Inscriptions of *Asoka*-Hultzsch. E. Hultzsch (ed.), *Corpus Inscriptionum Indicarum, I.*
JAOS.   *Journal of the American Oriental Society.*
JASB.   *Journal of the Asiatic Society of Bengal.*
Jat.   *Jataka.*
JBBRAS.   *Journal of the Bombay Branch of the Royal Asiatic Society.*
JBORS.   *Journal of the Bihar and Orissa Research Society.*
JIH.   *Journal of Indian History.*
JNSI.   *Journal of the Numismatic Society of India.*
JRAS.   *Journal of the Royal Asiatic Society of Great Britain and Ireland.*
M&S.   K. A. Nilakanta Sastri (ed.), *A Comprehensive History of India,* II, *The Mauryas and Satavahanas.*
MASI.   *Memoirs of the Archaeological Survey of India.*
MBH.   *Mahabharata.*
MDS.   *Manava Dharmashastra.*
MhV.   *Mahavamsa.*
MN.   *Majjhima Nikaya.*
MPE.   *Minor Pillar Edicts.*

N&M.	K. A. Nilakanta Sastri (ed.), *Age of the Nandas and Mauryas.*
PE.	*Pillar Edicts.*
PHAI.	H. C. Raychoudhuri, *Political History of Ancient India.*
RE.	*Rock Edicts.*
RV.	*Rig Veda.*
SamN.	*Samyutta Nikaya.*
SBE.	*Sacred Books of the East.*
SN.	*Sutta Nipata.*
SRE.	*Separate Rock Edicts.*
VDS.	*Vishnu Dharmashastra.*
Vin.	*Vinaya Texts.*

CHAPTER I

1. The date of Asoka's coronation is based on the acceptance of 487-486 B.C. as the year in which the Buddha passed away. The Buddhist Chronicles mention that Asoka's coronation took place in the 218th year after the Buddha's demise. The author has generally accepted the Buddhist tradition as authentic. For the authenticity of the Buddhist accounts of Asoka see R. K. Mookerji, "The Authenticity of Asokan Legends" in *Buddhistic Studies* edited by B. C. Law, pp. 547 ff.; for a discussion on the date of the Buddha's demise see *AIU*, p. 36; for a recent summary of various theories on the subject see Madan Mohan Singh, "The Date of Buddha Nirvana," *JIH*, XXXIX, iii, December 1961, pp. 359-363; also see R. Thapar, *Asoka and the Decline of the Mauryas*, p. 25 and P. H. L. Eggermont, *The Chronology of the Reign of Asoka Moriya*, pp. 142-143.

2. A phrase used by Arnold Toynbee in his *A Study of History*, I, 86-87.

3. *SN*, p. 13; also see D. D. Kosambi, *An Introduction to the Study of Indian History*, pp. 129 ff.

4. *CHI*, p. 194.

5. *Vin* II, 156; *SBE* XX, 187; for a sculptural representation of the scene see Barua and Sinha (eds.), *Barhut Inscriptions*, p. 59.

6. An old but still standard work on the subject of the guild system of ancient India is *Corporate Life in Ancient India* by R. C. Majumdar; also see A. N. Bose, *Social and Rural Economy of Northern India*, pp. 281 ff.; Kosambi, pp. 220-221; for relationships between the guilds and caste see Max Weber, *The Religion of India*, pp. 33-39.

7. For details of trade and trade routes see *N&M*, pp. 269-270.

8. For various types of bonded labor see D. R. Chanana, *Slavery in Ancient India*, pp. 55 ff.

9. For the Buddha's views on the caste system see *SN*, pp. 21-24, 80-85, 116-123; *MN*, II, 83-90, 147-157, 177-184.

10. For an account of the Achaemenid empire in India see A. T. Olmstead, *History of the Persian Empire*, (Achaemenid Period), pp. 144 ff.; *AIU*, pp. 39-43; *CHI*, pp. 295-306.

11. E. Ilief Robson (ed.), *Arrian, Anabasis of Alexander*, V, xv; II, 49.

12. *CHI*, p. 345 ff.; *AIU*, pp. 51-53; *N&M*, pp. 78-80.

13. *N&M*, p. 31.

14. P. Jouguet, *Macedonian Imperialism and the Hellenization of the East,* I, 182; N. R. Ray, *Maurya and Sunga Art,* p. 62.

15. But Kosambi places it in 320; *AIU,* p. 54, in 324; *M&S,* p. 5, in 323; *CHI,* p. 424, in 323 or 321.

16. *AIU,* p. 32.

17. *N&M,* p. 10.

18. *Samantapasadika,* (Commentary on *DN*), I, 10; also see N. A. Jayawicrame, *The Inception of Discipline and the Vinaya Pitaka,* p. 8.

19. *MhV,* V, 241-243; *Vamsatthappakasini* (Commentary on *MhV*), I, 183-186; *Mahabodhivamsa,* p. 91.

20. B. A. Saletore doubts if an actual war between Seleucus and Chandragrupta ever took place and dates the treaty between them at the end of 303 or early 302 B.C., *India's Diplomatic Relations with the West,* pp. 125 ff., 131.

21. Robson, II, 311.

22. See R. C. Majumdar, *Classical Accounts of India,* p. 193.

23. *AIU,* pp. 67-68.

24. *Ibid.*

CHAPTER II

1. *AIU,* p. 70.

2. B. M. Barua, *Asoka and His Inscriptions,* p. 35; Tishya was, for some time, appointed vice-regent by Asoka, *MhV,* V, 33.

3. See *M&S,* p. 19.

4. *Artha,* p. 9.

5. *Ibid.,* p. 8.

6. *Ibid.,* p 8.

7. *Ibid.,* p. 8.

8. See Daniel H. H. Ingalls, "Authority and Law in Ancient India," *JAOS,* Supplement No. 17, July-September, 1954, pp. 35-44.

9. For the suggestion that Asoka conquered Ujjayini see *Samantapasadika,* I, 45; also Barua, pp. 9, 35. Excavations at Taxila (Sirkap) have unearthed an inscription on a white marble pillar set up in honor of a high official called Romedote, in which there is a reference to Priyadarshin (Asoka), who must have been a governor there; see J. Marshall, *Guide to Taxila,* p. 74.

10. *AIU,* 606; H. G. Rawlinson, *Intercourse Between India and the Western World,* pp. 42-43.

11. *Saratthappakasini* (Commentary on *SamN*), I, 151.

12. *Artha,* pp. 6, 36-38, 449.

13. *MhV,* V, 259 ff.; *Thupavamsa,* p. 37; Marshall, p. 16, states that Asoka was a worshipper of Shiva without citing evidence on which this conclusion is based.

14. *RE,* IX, Ray, p. 69, argues that Asoka was against folk religious rites, popular religious demonstrations, and old socio-religious rites and practices. But this attitude could have developed after his conversion.

15. *RE,* V, XIII.

16. *Vamsatthappakasini,* I, 190.

17. H. Jacobi, "Jaina Sutras," *SBE,* XII, ix-xxii.

18. For an account of the Ajivika sect and its history see A. L. Basham, *History and Doctrines of the Ajivikas*, pp. 34 ff., 213 ff.

CHAPTER III

1. *Divya*, p. xxvi.
2. *Dipavamsa*, VI, 15-22.
3. For stories on Asoka's "hell" see Watters, *On Yuan Chwang's Travels in India*, II, 89.
4. See T. W. Rhys Davids, *Buddhist India* p. 280; R. K. Mookerji, *Chandragupta Maurya and His Times*, p. 73; V. A. Smith, *Asoka*, pp. 20-21; D. R. Bhandarkar rejects this interval, *Asoka*, p. 9.
5. *RE*, V, VI.
6. *Shatapatha Brahmana*, V, 2-3; *Aitareya Brahmana*, VIII, 15.
7. *N&M*, p. 20.
8. Bhandarkar, p. 29.
9. *AIU*, pp. 32-35.
10. Bhandarkar, p. 31.
11. Some authorities place the Nabhakas and Nabhapantis on the Indo-Nepalese Frontier, see *N&M*, pp. 222-223; Bhandarkar places the Pulindas in Madhya Pradesh, p. 35.
12. For the text of the inscription see P. H. L. Eggermont and J. Hoftijzer, *The Moral Edicts of Asoka*, pp. 42-45.
13. Barua, *Asoka and His Inscriptions*, II, 5.
14. *AIU*, pp. 1-62; *EI*, VIII, 64-65; Bhandarkar points out that the term *yavana* in the Rudradaman Inscription at Junagadh should be taken to mean "not a Greek but a Persian," *M&S*, p. 28, note.
15. *M&S*, pp. 69-70; Saletore argues that Deimachos was an ambassador sent by Seleucus Nicator, p. 134.
16. *M&S*, p. 26; Saletore identifies Turamaya with Ptolemy III (247-222 B.C.), the son and successor of Ptolemy Philadelphus, pp. 142-143.
17. *MhV*, Chapters VI and XII.
18. See J. Przyluski, *La Legende de l'Empereur Acoka*, pp. 283 ff.; Barua holds that the name Tishyarakshita is a fiction, that the Padmavati of the Sanskrit legend and Kuruvaki of the Queen's Edict are the same, and the "second queen," Devi and Asandhimitra are identical, p. 54.
19. *Separate Kalinga Edict; M&S*, p. 22.
20. *RE*, VI.
21. *RE*, I.
22. R. C. Majumdar (ed.), *The Classical Accounts of India*, p. 105.
23. *Artha*, p. 8.
24. Hultzsch, p. 47.
25. See *N&M*, p. 260.
26. Kosambi, p. 196.
27. *Artha*, p. 45.

CHAPTER IV

1. *RE*, XIII.
2. S. Radhakrishnan, *Dhammapada*, p. 94.

3. *MhV*, V, 68.

4. *Divya*, pp. 374-377.

5. The *DN* and *MN* contain a number of *suttas* with an autobiographical content, and these have been used along with parts of *Vin* I to reconstruct this part of the Buddha's life; also see E. J. Thomas, *The Life of the Buddha as Legend and History*, pp. 16 ff.

6. See A. B. Keith, *Religion and Philosophy of the Veda*, I, 257 ff.

7. See S. Radhakrishnan, *The Principal Upanisads*, pp. 52 ff.

8. *DN*, I, 9, 215-220; *MN*, I, 426-431.

9. *Vin*, I, 4.

10. For the religion of the Buddhist layman see the author's *Buddhism and Asoka*, pp. 25 ff.

11. *Samchi Edict;* for a history of the rise of the sects see N. Dutt, *Early History of the Spread of Buddhism and the Buddhist Schools*, pp. 197 ff.

12. Hultzsch, pp. 167, 169.

13. For a discussion on the terms see B. C. Law, *IC*, I, 123; Bhandarkar, p. 80.

14. See J. Fleet in *JRAS*, 1908, p. 496.

15. See *RE*, I; *PE*, V.

16. P. H. L. Eggermont and J. Hoftijzer, *The Moral Edicts of Asoka*, p. 45.

17. P. H. L. Eggermont, *The Chronology of the Reign of Asoka Moriya*, pp. 73-74.

18. See *M&S*, p. 751.

19. *DN*, II, 2-3.

20. *Rummindei PE*.

21. Hultzsch, p. 173.

22. J. Marshall, *Guide to Taxila*, p. 16; S. Beal, *Travels of Hiuen-Thsang*, II, 245-246.

23. S. Bhattacharya, *Select Asokan Epigraphs*, pp. 79-80.

24. For a discussion on the historicity of the councils see H. Oldenberg, *Vin*, I, xxi ff.; Bhandarkar, p. 95; R. K. Mookerji, *Asoka*, p. 67; H. Kern, *Manual of Buddhism*, p. 11; R. Pischel, *Leben und Lehre des Buddha*, p. 103.

25. T. W. Rhys Davids, *Buddhist India*, pp. 298-299.

26. *PE*, IV.

CHAPTER V

1. John W. Spellman argues that the concept of the righteous emperor (*cakkavatti*) was inspired "in part" by the reforms of Asoka, *Political Theory of Ancient India*, p. 175; this does not seem to be correct since long before the time of Asoka the ideal of the righteous world-conquerer was known in Buddhist as well as Brahmanical traditions. For the Buddhist ideas see *DN*, II, p. 16.

2. See U. N. Ghoshal, *A History of Indian Political Ideas*, pp. 53, 255.

3. *SRE*-Dhauli, I & II; Hultzsch, pp. 95, 98.

4. For Asoka's ideas see *PE*, IV; *SRE*-Jaugada, II; Hultzsch, p. 112, l. 7 R; *Artha*, p. 38.

5. *SN*, pp. 51, 52-53, 54, 119.

6. See S. P. Sinha, "Position of the Brahmanas in Mauryan Times," *Indian History Congress, Proceedings of the Sixteenth Session* (1953), p. 98.

7. *Artha*, p. 47.

8. S. Beal, III, pp. 322-326.

9. Hultzsch, pp. 12-13; V. R. R. Dikshitar points out that some of these reporters were also informers supplying information on neighboring states, *Mauryan Polity*, p. 181.

10. *Artha*, pp. 36-39.

11. *RE*, III.

12. *Artha*, p. 12.

13. *Divya*, pp. 372-373, 384.

14. For a discussion on the Buddhist ideals of the state see the author's paper on "Dhammiko Dhammaraja" in *Indica*, pp. 161-165.

15. See *RE*, II, IX, XI; *PE*, IV, V, VII, VIII.

16. *Vin*, I, 76; II, 271.

17. Robson, II, 339-341, 353-355.

18. *Artha*, pp. 146-150; for the role of cavalry in ancient Indian warfare see B. P. Sinha, "Art of War in Ancient India," *Journal of World History*, IV, i, (1957), 136-140.

19. *Artha*, p. 399.

20. R. K. Mookerji, *Chandragupta Maurya and His Times*, p. 165.

21. See M. H. Gopal, *Mauryan Public Finance*, pp. 195-197.

22. *PE*, IV.

23. R. G. Basak, *Asokan Inscriptions*, p. 96; Smith, *Asoka*, p. 185; Dikshitar, *Mauryan Polity*, p. 218; *M&S*, p. 28.

24. Dhandarkar, p. 53; *M&S*, p. 19.

25. Hultzsch, pp. 56-57.

26. See Basham, pp. 146-149.

27. *MRE*, I, II.

28. *RE*, XII.

29. *PE*, VII; *MRE*, II.

30. *Artha*, pp. 160 ff.; *SRE*-Kalinga; Bhandarkar, p. 58.

31. Rawlinson, pp. 56 ff.; Mookerji, *Chandragupta Maurya and His Times*, pp. 143-44.

32. See H. N. Sinha, *Sovereignty in Ancient Indian Polity*, pp. 133 ff., 192; C. Drekmeir, *Kingship and Community in Early India*, pp. 169-172.

33. *RE*, XII.

CHAPTER VI

1. For Kautalyan philosophy see *Artha*, pp. 8, 293 ff.; U. N. Ghoshal, *A History of Indian Political Ideas*, pp. 554, 558; M. V. Krishna Rao, *Studies in Kautilya*, pp. 48-56; C. Drekmeir, *Kingship and Community in Early India*, pp. 289 ff.

2. N. A. Nikam and R. McKeon (eds.), *The Edicts of Asoka*, p. viii.

3. Saletore, pp. 144-145.

4. See *RE*, VII, IX; *MRE*, I; *AngN*, III, 149; *Jat*, III, 212; V 479, 488; VI, 151.

5. For the Brahmanical theories on the origins of the state see *Taittiriya Brahmana*, I, 2, 2, 2; *Mbh*, XII, 58, 12-16; for the Buddhist views see *DN*, III, 84-93.

6. *RE*, V.

7. *RE*, VII, IX, XII.

8. *AngN*, III, 151.

9. Nikam and McKeon, p. ix.

10. *Artha*, pp. 411-412; Dikshitar, *Mauryan Polity*, p. 129.

11. Hultzsch, pp. 133-134.

12. Ghoshal, p. 292; Drekmeir, pp. 289-290; Dikshitar, p. 92; *SRE*-Dhauli; *MRE*, II; *DN*, II, 72 ff.

13. For the Buddhist views on sacrifice see *MN*, I, 344; *Dhp*, VIII, 7; S. Radhakrishnan, *Dhammapada*, p. 95.

14. Hultzsch, p. 21.

15. *Ibid.*, p. 121.

16. *Dhp*, XIX, 6; XIV, 5; IV, 10.

17. But for a different view see Henry S. Albinski, "The Place of the Emperor Asoka in Ancient Indian Political Thought," *Midwest Journal of Political Science*, II, I (February 1958), 71.

18. Hultzsch, p. 17.

19. *RE*, IX; *MRE*, I; *PE*, II, IV; *SRE*-Kalinga I.

20. *DN*, III, 182 ff.

21. *Sarnath, Kaushambi,* and *Samchi Edicts.*

22. Kosambi, pp. 193-199, 224-225.

CHAPTER VII

1. R. C. Majumdar, *The Classical Accounts of India*, p. 257.

2. J. Marshall, *Guide to Taxila*, p. 13.

3. Robson, pp. 353, 357.

4. *Artha*, p. 232; B. N. Puri, *India in the Time of Patanjali*, pp. 128-129.

5. Majumdar, pp. 225, 227.

6. *Ibid.*, pp. 224-225.

7. For slavery in ancient India through the various ages see J. Marshall, *Mohenjo-Daro and the Indus Civilization*, I, 92; S. Piggott, *Prehistoric India*, p. 170; *RV*, I, 126; VIII, 56, 3; X, 86, 5; *Jat*, VI, 285; VI, 577; *Artha*, pp. 205 ff.; for forced labor in ancient India see R. Choudhary, "Visti in Ancient India," *IHQ*, XXXVIII, 1 (March 1962), 44-59.

8. Majumdar, p. 225.

9. See *RE*, XIII; Max Weber, *The Religion of India*, pp. 11 ff.; Kosambi, pp. 24-25; Drekmeir, pp. 79-80; for untouchability in the pre-Mauryan age see R. S. Sharma, *Sudras in Ancient India*, p. 126.

10. Majumdar, p. 231.

11. *Mahabhashya*, III, 2, 8.

12. Om Prakash, *Food and Drink in Ancient India*, p. 87; *Artha*, pp. 131 ff.

13. *Mahabhashya*, I, 25; Majumdar, p. 231.

14. *Jat*, I, 112, 120, 195, 478; III, 448; IV, 106-107; VI, 346.

15. *Artha*, pp. 89 ff.

16. See Puri, pp. 131-135.

17. For such studies see Allan, *Catalogue of the Coins of Ancient India;* Rapson, *Indian Coins;* Durga Prasad, *JASB, Numismatic Supplement,* XXX; Kosambi, *JBBRAS,* XXIV-XXV; Dani, *JNSI, XVII,* II; *MASI,* No: 59.

18. See R. B. Pandey, *Indian Paleography,* pp. 18 ff.; C. S. Upsak, *The History and Paleography of Mauryan Brahmi Script,* pp. 5-15; A. H. Dani argues that the "Indian Brahmi was created on the basis of the North Semitic letters. But Brahmi is not a slavish adoption of the North Semitic signs. There is considerable local genius visible in its formation," *Indian Paleography,* pp. 28-29.

19. A. B. Keith states that Panini cannot be later than the third century B.C. but not much earlier than the fourth century B.C.; see *Religion and Philosophy of the Veda,* I, 20, note 1.

20. J. Vogel, *Buddhist Art in India, Ceylon and Java,* p. 10.

21. Marshall and Foucher, *The Monuments of Samchi,* I, 21.

22. For details see *M&S,* pp. 89-90; *AIU,* pp. 495-498; A. K. Coomaraswamy, *History of Indian and Indonesian Art,* p. 18.

23. *CHI,* p. 575.

24. N. R. Ray, *Maurya and Sunga Art,* pp. 6, 26-27, 28.

25. In a new interpretation of the phrase *sila vigadabhica* S. Parnavitana suggests that Asoka's purpose was to mark the exact spot of the Buddha's birthplace and promote the welfare of his people in this world and the next by enabling them to visit the exact spot; *JAOS,* 82, No. 2 (April-June 1962), pp. 164-167.

26. J. P. Vogel, *The Goose in Indian Literature and Art,* pp. 1-12.

27. Ray, pp. 31, 41, 55.

28. B. Rowland, *The Art and Architecture of India,* p. 43; see also Ray, pp. 31, 59.

29. Rowland, p. 5.

30. For Mauryan terracottas see C. C. Dasgupta, *Origin and Evolution of Indian Clay Sculpture,* pp. 139-159.

31. For details on pottery see Wheeler and Krishna Deva in *Ancient India,* I, 55, IX, 119, 142.

32. For discussions on the decline and fall of the Mauryas see Bhandarkar, *Asoka,* pp. 237, 244, 256; Raychoudhuri, *PHAI,* pp. 236, 304; Jayaswal, *JBORS,* II, 8; Mookerji in his introduction to *Early History of Kausambi* (by Ghose), p. xii; Harprasad Sastri, *JASB,* 1910, pp. 259-262; Gokhale, *Buddhism and Asoka,* pp. 143-148.

A Select Bibliography

ASOKAN INSCRIPTIONS

Barua, B. M., *Asoka and His Inscriptions*, Calcutta, 1948.
Barua, B. M., *Inscriptions of Asoka*, Part II, Calcutta, 1943.
Basak, R. G., *Asokan Inscriptions*, Calcutta, 1959.
Bhandarkar, D. R. and Majumdar, S. N., *Inscriptions of Asoka*, Calcutta, 1920.
Bhattacharya, S., *Select Asokan Epigraphs*, Calcutta, 1952.
Bloch, J., *Les Inscriptions d'Asoka*, Paris, 1913.
Eggermont, P. H. L. and Hoftijzer, J., *The Moral Edicts of Asoka*, Leiden, 1962.
Hultzsch, E., *Corpus Inscriptionum Indicarum*, I, *Inscriptions of Asoka*, Oxford, 1925.
Murti, G. S. and Aiyangar, A. N. K., *The Edicts of Asoka Priyadarsin*, Madras, 1951.
Nikam, K. A. and McKeon, R., *The Edicts of Asoka*, Chicago, 1959.
Sen, A. C., *Asoka's Edicts*, Calcutta, 1956.
Senart, E., *Les Inscriptions de Piyadassi*, Paris, 1881.
Sircar, D. C., *Select Inscriptions bearing on Indian History and Civilization*, Calcutta, 1942.
Woolner, A. C., *Asoka, Text and Glossary*, Calcutta, 1924.

PALI AND SANKRIT LITERATURE

Anguttara Nikaya, edited by Morris and Hardy, I-IV, London, 1885-1888; translated as *Gradual Sayings* by Woodward, I-V, London, 1952-1956.
Digha Nikaya, edited by T. W. Rhys Davids and J. E. Carpenter, I-III, London, 1890-1911; translated as *Dialogues of the Buddha*, by T. W. & C. A. F. Rhys Davids, I-III, London, 1956-1959.
Dipavamsa, edited and translated by H. Oldenberg, London, 1897.
Jataka, edited by V. Fausboll, I-VII, London, 1877-1897; translated by various hands, I-VII, London, 1895-1903.
Keith, A. B., *History of Sanskrit Literature*, Oxford, 1928.
Law, B. C., *History of Pali Literature*, I-II, London, 1933.
Mahabharata, edited by Krishnacharya and Vyasacharya, Bombay, 1906-1909; translated by M. N. Dutt, Calcutta, 1895-1903.
Mahavamsa, edited and translated by W. Geiger, London, 1908-1912.
Majjhima Nikaya, edited by Trenckner, Chalmers and Rhys Davids, I-III, London, 1888-1925; translated by Woodward and Horner as *Middle Length Sayings*, London, 1954-1959.

Malalsekera, G. P., *Dictionary of Pali Proper Names*, I-II, London, 1937-1938.
Malalsekera, G. P., *The Pali Literature of Ceylon*, London, 1928.
Manavadharmashastra, edited by J. Jolly, London, 1887 and translated by G. Buhler, *S.B.E.*, XXV, Oxford, 1886.
Mudrarakshasa of Vishakhadatta, edited by M. R. Kale, Bombay, 1916.
Radhakrishnan, S., *The Bhagavadgita*, New York, 1956.
Radhakrishnan, S., *The Dhammapada*, London, 1950.
Samyutta Nikaya, edited by Leon Freer, I-IV, London, 1884-1894; translated as *Kindred Sayings* by Woodward and Rhys Davids, I-III, London, 1917-1924.
Sutta Nipata, edited by D. Andersen and H. Smith, London, 1913.
Thera-Theri Gatha, edited by Oldenberg and Pischell, London, 1883, translated as *Psalms of the Early Buddhists-Brethren-Sisters* by Rhys Davids, London, 1913.
Vinaya Pitakam, edited by H. Oldenberg, I-IV, London, 1879-1883.
Winternitz, M., *History of Indian Literature*, I-II, Calcutta, 1927-1937.

MODERN WORKS ON ASOKA AND THE MAURYAS

Bhandarkar, D. R., *Asoka*, Calcutta, 1925.
Eggermont, P. H. L., *The Chronology of the Reign of Asoka Moriya*, Leiden, 1956.
Gokhale, B. G., *Buddhism and Asoka*, Baroda, 1949.
Kern, F., *Asoka, Kaiser und Missionar*, Bern, 1956.
McPhail, J. M., *Asoka*, Calcutta, 1926.
Mookerji, R. K., *Asoka*, Delhi, 1962.
Przyluski, J., *La Legende de l'Empereur Acoka*, Paris, 1923.
Smith, V. A., *Asoka*, Delhi, 1957.
Thapar, R., *Asoka and the Decline of the Mauryas*, London, 1961.

GENERAL HISTORIES

Aiyangar, S. K., *Ancient India and South Indian History and Culture*, 2 vols., Poona, 1941.
Bhargava, P. L., *Chandragupta Maurya*, Lucknow, 1935.
Kosambi, D. D., *Introduction to the Study of Indian History*, Bombay, 1956.
La Vallee Poussin, L. de, *L'Inde aux temps des Mauryas*, Paris, 1930.
Majumdar, R. C. and Pusalkar, A. D., *History and Culture of the Indian People, The Age of Imperial Unity*, Bombay, 1951.
Mookerji, R. K., *Chandragupta Maurya and His Times*, Madras, 1943.
Nilakanta Sastri, K. A., *Age of the Nandas and Mauryas*, Banaras, 1952.
Nilakanta Sastri, K. A., *A Comprehensive History of India*, II, *The Mauryas and Satavahanas*, Bombay, 1957.
Olmstead, A. T., *History of the Persian Empire*, Chicago, 1949.
Pargiter, F. E., *The Purana Text of the Dynasties of the Kali Age*, London 1913.
Pargiter, F. E., *Ancient Indian Historical Tradition*, London, 1922.
Rapson, E. J., *Cambridge History of India*, I, Delhi, 1962.
Rawlinson, H. G., *Intercourse between India and the Western World*, Cambridge, 1916.

Raychoudhuri, H. C., *Political History of Ancient India*, Calcutta, 1950.
Sircar, D. C., *Studies in the Geography of Ancient and Medieval India*, Delhi, 1960.
Smith, V. A., *Early History of India*, Oxford, 1924.
Saletore, B. A., *India's Diplomatic Relations with the West*, Bombay, 1958.
Tarn, W. W., *Hellenistic Civilization*, London, 1927.
Tarn, W. W., *The Greeks in Bactria and India*, Cambridge, 1951.

ART, ARCHAEOLOGY, NUMISMATICS, PALAEOGRAPHY

Allen, J., *Catalogue of the Coins of Ancient India* (in the British Museum), London, 1936.
Coomaraswamy, A. K., *History of Indian and Indonesian Art*, London, 1927.
Dani, A. H., *Indian Palaeography*, Oxford, 1963.
Dasgupta, C. C., *Origin and Evolution of Indian Clay Sculpture*, Calcutta, 1961.
Foucher, A., *The Beginnings of Buddhist Art*, Paris, 1917.
Grunwedel, A., *Buddhist Art in India*, London, 1901.
Gupta, P. L., *A Bibliography of the Hoard of Punch-Marked Coins in Ancient India*, Bombay, 1955.
Kuraishi, M. H., *A Guide to Rajgir*, Delhi, 1939.
Marshall, J., *A Guide to Taxila*, Cambridge, 1960.
Pandey, R. B., *Indian Paleography*, Banaras, 1952.
Ray, N. R., *Maurya and Sunga Art*, Calcutta, 1945.
Rowland, B., *The Art and Architecture of India*, London, 1953.
Smith, V. A., *History of Fine Art in India and Ceylon*, Oxford, 1930.
Upsak, C. S., *The History and Paleography of Mauryan Brahmi Script*, Nalanda, Patna, 1960.
Vogel, J. P., *Buddhist Art in India*, Oxford, 1936.
Zimmer, H., *The Art of Indian Asia*, New York, 1955.

POLITY

Altekar, A. S., *State and Government in Ancient India*, Banaras, 1949.
Bandopadhyaya, N. C., *Development of Hindu Polity and Political Theories*, 2 parts, Calcutta, 1927-1938.
Beni Parasad, *The State in Ancient India*, Allahabad, 1928.
Bhandarkar, D. R., *Some Aspects of Ancient Hindu Polity*, Banaras, 1929.
Brelser, B., *Kautilya Studien*, Bonn, 1927-1934.
Dikshitar, V. R. R., *Mauryan Polity*, Madras, 1932.
Drekmeir, C., *Kingship and Community in Early India*, Stanford, 1962.
Ghoshal, U. N., *A History of Indian Political Ideas*, Bombay, 1959.
Gopal, M. H., *Mauryan Public Finance*, London, 1935.
Hocart, A. M., *Kings and Councillors*, Cairo, 1936.
Hocart, A. M., *Kingship*, London, 1927.
Jayaswal, K. P., *Hindu Polity*, Bangalore, 1955.
Jolly, J., *Arthasastra of Kautilya*, Lahore, 1923.
Konow, S., *Kautilya Studien*, Oslo, 1945.
Krishna Rao, M. V., *Studies in Kautilya*, Mysore, 1953.

Law, N. N., *Aspects of Ancient Indian Polity*, Oxford, 1921.
Mookerji, R. K., *Local Government in Ancient India*, Oxford, 1920.
Rau, W., *Staat und Gesselschaft im Alten Indien*, Wiesbaden, 1957.
Sen, A. K., *Studies in Hindu Political Thought*, Calcutta, 1926.
Shamasastry, R., *Kautilya Arthasastra*, Mysore, 1924; translation, Mysore, 1956.
Sharma, R. S. *Aspects of Political Ideas and Institutions in Ancient India*, Delhi, 1959.
Sinha, H. N., *Sovereignty in Ancient India*, London, 1938.
Spellman, J. W., *Political Theory of Ancient India*, Oxford, 1964.
Stein, O., *Megasthenes und Kautilya*, Wien, 1921.

RELIGIONS AND PHILOSOPHIES

Basham, A. L., *History and Doctrines of the Ajivikas*, London, 1951.
Coomaraswamy, A. K., *Buddha and the Gospel of Buddhism*, London, 1928.
Dasgupta, S. N., *A History of Indian Philosophy*, Calcutta, 1922-1955.
Dutt, N., *Early Monastic Buddhism*, Calcutta, 1941-1945.
Dutt, S., *Early Buddhism Monachism*, London, 1924.
Von Glassenapp, H., *Der Jainismus*, Berlin, 1926.
Gokhale, B. G., *Indian Thought Through the Ages*, A Study of some Dominant Concepts, New York, 1961.
Horner, I. B., *The Early Buddhist Theory of Man Perfected*, London, 1936.
Keith, A. B., *Religion and Philosophy of the Veda*, 2 vols., Cambridge, Mass., 1925.
Kane, P. V., *History of Dharmasastra*, I-IV, Poona, 1930-1946.
Pande, G. C., *Studies in the Origin of Buddhism*, Allahabad, 1957.
Radhakrishnan, S., *Philosophy of the Upanishads*, London, 1935.
Radhakrishnan, S., *Indian Philosophy*, 2 vols., London, 1923-1927.
Rhys Davids, T. W., *Buddhism*, London, 1907.
Schubring, W., *Die Lehre der Jainas*, Gottingen, 1926.
Shah, C. J., *Jainism in Northern India*, Bombay, 1932.
Oldenberg, H., *Buddha, His Life, His Doctrine, His Order*, London, 1882.
Thomas, E. J., *The History of Buddhist Thought*, London, 1933.
Weber, M., *The Religion of India*, Glencoe, 1960.
Zimmer, H., *Philosophies of India*, New York, 1959.

SOCIAL AND ECONOMIC CONDITIONS

Agarwala, V. S., *India as known to Panini*, Lucknow, 1953.
Arrianus, Flavius, Arrian, with an English translation by E. Illief Robson, 2 vols., London, 1929.
Bose, A., *Social and Rural Economy of Northern India*, Calcutta, 1942-1945.
Das, S. K., *Economic History of Ancient India*, Calcutta, 1925.
Fick, R., *The Social Organization in North-East India in Buddha's Time*, Calcutta, 1920.
Horner, I. B., *Women under Primitive Buddhism*, London, 1930.
Law, B. C., *India as Described in the Early Texts of Buddhism and Jainism*, London, 1941.
Majumdar, R. C., *Corporate Life in Ancient India*, Poona, 1922.
Majumdar, R. C., *The Classical Accounts of India*, Calcutta, 1960.

McCrindle, J. W., *Ancient India as described by Megasthenes and Arrian,* Calcutta, 1960.

Mehta, R. L., *Pre-Buddhist India,* Bombay, 1939.

Mookerji, R. K., *A History of Indian Shipping,* Allahabad, 1962.

Om Prakash, *Food and Drink in Ancient India,* Delhi, 1961.

Pran Nath, *A Study in the Economic Condition of Ancient India,* London, 1929.

Puri, B. N., *India in the Time of Patanjali,* Bombay, 1957.

Rhys Davids, T. W., *Buddhist India,* London, 1903.

Rostovtzeff, M. I., *The Social and Economic History of the Hellenistic World,* Oxford, 1941.

Sharma, R. S., *Sudras in Ancient India,* Patna, 1958.

Warmington, E. H., *Commerce between the Roman Empire and India,* Cambridge, 1928.

Index and Glossary